The Successful Writer's Guide to

Publishing

Magazine

Articles

Eva Shaw, Ph.D.

The Successful Writer's Guide to Publishing Magazine Articles is the perfect prescription for any writer. It is motivational and practical medicine, that one can take and apply today. Eva is filled with warmth, honesty, and lots of knowledge. So is this book. Eva's teaching style is fast-paced, pertinent, high energy and creative. Her insight and giving spirit is a breath of fresh air that fills you with fire and desire, for more and more.

C. J. Johnson, M.A. Therapist and writer
Atlanta, Georgia

———————————

Drawing principles from her vast personal knowledge, Eva is able to guide the novice and experienced from the guess work of trial and error to the surety of confident professionalism. Her clear, practical, and easy-to-follow advice is absolutely invaluable. Now, 16 magazine articles, two books and three years, I have to thank her.

Heather Down, elementary school teacher and writer,
Toronto, Ontario, Canada

———————————

Eva's writing tips are clear and practical. She outlines everything the aspiring or experienced writer needs to know to sell magazine articles. Her creative ideas will not only motivate you, but help you market and place your magazine articles. If you want to be published, read this comprehensive writing guide.

Carol T. Beekman, columnist, OC METRO Magazine,
Laguna Niguel, California

———————————

By following Eva Shaw's methods, a seed of an idea will soon become a published magazine article. Not only does she instruct you on how to get an article published, she has a way of inspiring that often elusive creative spark all writers need from time to time.

Jackie Landis, editor, ghostwriter, writer,
San Diego, California

———————————

I owe my new-found career as a freelance writer to Eva Shaw. By using the bubble method I am able to develop ideas for dozens of different articles. Follow the suggestions in her book, and a career writing for magazines is yours!

Teri Thomas, Flight Attendant and Freelance Writer
Dana Point, CA

We at *San Diego Writers' Monthly* magazine know all too well what a writing treasure Eva Shaw is and has been for many years. *The Successful Writer's Guide to Publishing Magazine Articles*, another of her reader-friendly gems, is a must-read for any aspiring OR professional writer. She's just that good!

Mike MacCarthy, Publisher,
San Diego Writers' Monthly
San Diego, California

I had four solid magazine articles planned and information on where and how to market them before leaving Eva Shaw's class. Writing for religious publications, I knew I had hundreds of inspirational ideas, but Eva showed me how to make them marketable. Her book was the best investment for my career.

Eva Shaw tells you what, shows you how, and then tells you why. Teaching at the NWA conference recently, she held the class in her hand. With humor and common sense, she teaches how to make a good idea into a marketable one. Her book gave me a new perspective on submitting for inspirational publications.

Eva Shaw is a petite package of fireworks. I attended her exciting class at a NWA conference. Eva showed me practical ways of making my ideas marketable. She encouraged, "If you work better keeping your idea files in a milk crate, then do it!" Reading her book opened a new avenue for my inspirational writing.

Lynda S. Harvey, President
H.E.A.R.T Studios, Thornton, Colorado

Shaw's methods of writing and research will get you published well ahead of other writers. If you want your "ship to come in," let Eva Shaw launch your career and help you navigate. She's a lighthouse of information and her writing talents and mentoring will move you out of the fog and swiftly into clear blue waters, cause she's "wind to your sails." Eva Shaw's ability to know which way the publishing winds are blowing is uncanny. *The Successful Writer's Guide to Publishing Magazine Articles* is the best!

Bill Stafford
Financial and Marketing Consultant
Riverside, California

As an author of hundreds of published articles, I find Eva Shaw an effective and inspiring example. Her enthusiasm is contagious. The techniques she suggests for releasing creative energy and for producing quality work are simple. Most important, THEY WORK!!

Gerald Kinro, Author of
That Which Does Not Kill Me Makes Me Stronger
Kanehoe, Hawaii

––––––––––––

Eva Shaw with *The Successful Writer's Guide to Publishing Magazine Articles* managed to crack the closet door open where a part of me was stuffed away for years by real-life practicalities and disappointments. She has this talent for making you want to go run around in the rain and jump in mud puddles. And the amazing thing is, it makes me want to write... and to dream, and do such "impractical" things but feel all bubbly inside like I could write a novel in the process. I would say she inspired and pushed me to "go for it."

Mary C. Harper
San Diego, California

––––––––––––

"Eva is a consummate writer and instructor. Her technique comes from the "hard knocks school" of writing, in which practical experience dominates theory. Eva is a wonderful combination of enthusiasm, real world experience and business acumen. Her tips and suggestions work."

Marion Foerster, Bibliographic Instruction Librarian
MiraCosta College
Oceanside, California

––––––––––––

Eva Shaw is a great example of a successful writer. Writers at all stages of their careers will benefit from her expert advice.

Sharon Goldinger
Senior Editor
PeopleSpeak

The Successful Writer's Guide to

Publishing Magazine Articles

by

Eva Shaw, Ph.D.

Loveland Press, LLC

Book Publishers
Loveland, Colorado

Copyright © 1998 by Eva Shaw

ISBN 0-9662696-1-6

First Edition 1998
Fourth Printing June, 2003

Printed in the United States of America

*The Successful Writer's Guide to Publishing
Magazine Articles* is published by:

Loveland Press
P.O. Box 7001
Loveland, CO 80537-0001
970/593-9557

Production Credits:

Edited by Barbara Teel
Cover Photo by CeCe Canton
Cover Concept by Char Campbell
Cover, Text Design, and Production by Ben Teel, Teel & Co.

Library of Congress Cataloging-in-Publication Data

Shaw, Eva, 1947–
    The successful writer's guide to publishing magazine articles / by
Eva Shaw. --1st ed.
        p.   cm.
    Includes bibliographical references and index.
    ISBN 0-9662696-1-6 (trade pbk. : alk. paper)
    1. Journalism--Authorship--Vocational guidance. 2. Feature
writing--Vocational guidance. I. Title.
PN147.S463 1998
808' .0667--dc21   98-33808
                                                                CIP

DEDICATION

To Zippy, as always.

A NOTE FROM
THE PUBLISHER

T his book has wide margins for a reason. Make notes, scribble a thought, write an address—anything—JUST USE THEM. This is your guide to being a successful writer; it should be filled with your personal additions to the text for your reference. You don't need a plug-in to use this tool. You can open it up anytime, anywhere, and read, make notes and gain further insight. Scribble, dog-ear the pages, use highlighters–whatever it takes—but convert it all to Queries, and Sales!

Luck is what happens when PREPARATION meets OPPORTUNITY.

— Darrell Royal

BIOGRAPHY

*A*n educator and advocate for issues concerning families, Eva Shaw, Ph.D., is the author of more than 1000 magazine articles and over 35 published books, many garnering her awards. She's the author of the bestselling *For the Love of Children*, Health Communications, and she teaches writing at the University of California and at conferences and workshops around the country. She lives with her husband, Joe, in Carlsbad, California, and in her spare time works in the garden, hikes, and volunteers with a myriad of organizations.

Contents

ACKNOWLEDGMENTS

My biggest fan continues to be there figuring out how to make it all work and in ingenious ways: Thank you my dearest Joe, husband, friend, manager, and creative genius. Thanks to Craig Nelsen who saw the merit of this book and others in the series. His ideas are constantly on target and I marvel at the speed of his insightful brain. And thank you and special hugs to all my writing students and those who have told me that my "system" works. This one's for each of you.

INTRODUCTION

*H*ave you ever thought about writing for magazines? Dreamed of interviewing celebrities? Creating articles about cutting edge topics? Or writing what's in your heart or your head? In your hands now is the key to making that dream a reality.

The Successful Writer's Guide to Publishing Magazine Articles outlines the methods to make your writing dreams come true. Sure there's a catch. You need a desire to be a writer and a sprinkle of creativity. It helps if you can compose a sentence, too, yet whether you have a Ph.D. from the school of hard knocks or Columbia University, you can be a magazine writer.

And a well-paid one at that. You can write part-time, in your spare time, or full-time. As a magazine writer you make your own hours, set your goals, and work when you want. You can work as hard as you want or do it in your leisure. You can plan your future with writing or plan to write for magazines after retirement.

I have been writing for magazines for nearly 20 years and have never regretted the decision. As someone who enjoys a good challenge, the profession is perfect for me. Every day is different and that makes me happy. On Monday I might write a how-to article about stretches for walkers. On Tuesday and Wednesday, I might write a food and cooking article on low-fat snacks. Thursday's writing could include a travel article. Friday I might write an inspirational piece for a spiritual publication. Writing for magazines is never boring.

How to use this book

Read through the book at your own speed and pick out what you need right now. I have taught thousands to use the methods that are included here so you're in good company. The concepts are easy to grasp and quick to apply. My students from the university and workshop classes who have used the techniques in this book have their work published. It's as simple as that.

If you're a seasoned writer and need specific tips, flip to the index. If you're just getting your feet wet, you'll want to use the book to have a strong foundation. I've written this so you can get the facts and put those manuscripts and queries in the mail.

Why wait? Turn your dreams into bylines in magazines and help yourself to a bright writing future as a magazine writer.

When is the best time to start writing for magazines? Now.

One

You Can
Write for Magazines

T hunder Alley. Llamas. Dirt Rag. VeloNews. Kalliope. SageWoman. Do the names of these magazines stir your imagination? The great news is that publications like these and others are looking for you.

There's no e-mail or phone message saying: "Lee Jones needed by *Vogue*," or "Chris Sanchez contact *Sports Illustrated*." That isn't necessary since editors' needs are authenticated each time the publication is printed. Editors need writers for well-written articles, essays, opinion pieces, fillers and information columns that you and I supply.

Freelancing has never been more lucrative. That's a controversial statement because there are doomsayers who spout, "My goodness—I can't remember when it's been such a tough market!" Yet for an energetic, determined, success-driven writer who knows how to weave words crisply and cleverly, the market is excellent.

Where do you fit in? Whether you're still waiting for that first acceptance or you've been around the "publishing block" a few hundred times, there are magazines "out there" waiting for your work. The trick is to match your ideas and writing style with the needs of magazine editors. That's exactly the goal of this book—and my goal as a university writing instructor and fellow freelance writer—to help you make a good match.

Matchmaker, matchmaker, find me a match? Yes, you'll have to do the work, yet by following some simple guidelines (all found within these pages), the success outlook is spectacular. With nearly 13,000 publications looking for writers, the chances for publication aren't just good, they're great. Conversely, by ignoring the tricks of the magazine writing trade, frustration could undermine a match made in magazine heaven.

More than ever, magazines are flourishing in the United States and abroad. Nonfiction articles are their lifeblood, and editors chase after writers who can produce provocative, timely, and entertaining copy to fill the pages of their publications. Editors want writers who can produce clear, consistently interesting, and entertaining copy.

What sells? You name it. In the years since I first began teaching how to write and sell magazine articles, and my writing books first came to print, styles have changed. There are new crazes, innovative concepts, and different styles in magazine writing. Why how many of us, ten years ago, could imagine the possibility of reading or writing for a magazine only published on the World Wide Web? Using the Internet to contact editors? Sending articles or queries via a contraption connected to the telephone? Even owning a fax machine?

These and scores of other reasons are why I've updated this ever-popular edition. Times have changed and freelance writers must change with them. If you currently own the original edition of this book, skim through this version. You'll notice it's had more than a face lift—it's had a total renovation.

As with the original edition, the book is slanted to the skillful, determined writer. It removes the guesswork and provides an understandable plan to sell every article produced. This edition also includes specific techniques for writing articles, from food articles to travel articles, Q&A's to the ever-popular how-to/self-help pieces.

For about twenty years I have made a very good living writing. I've written nonfiction articles for magazines, including the trade magazines, international periodicals, weekly newspapers and the tabloids. My articles have appeared in such diverse periodicals as the wholesome family newsmagazine *Grit* to the tantalizing, sometimes controversial *National Examiner*, plus plenty of publications such as *Weight Watchers Magazine, Woman, Dog Fancy, Shape, Modern Romance, Let's Live, Today's OR Nurse, American Fitness, Jewish Journal, Spa News, Westways, Essence,* and *Surfer.* Included on my list of credits are the articles written for trade magazines including *Stylist, Equal Opportunity, Ranch Dog, Recommend, Innkeeping World, Spa Specs,* and *Salon Today.* I also teach writing through the University of California's popular extension writing programs and at writers' conferences and events, and I'm a frequent guest lecturer and expert on television and radio. I love to share information about writing with anyone who has a desire to write and sell.

This is the book I wish I could have read years ago when I stopped talking about writing for magazines and got serious. I wanted to write for the magazines I'd been buying, reading, and dreaming of breaking into. At that time, I felt alone—I didn't even know a "real writer."

Within these pages are the tricks and tactics to help you write and sell nonfiction magazine articles. These are real world sales and success techniques.

Consider this book your road map to the constantly changing, ever challenging, completely addictive thrill of writing and selling articles and fillers.

If you're rethinking your future, if you're a determined, yet so far unpublished writer, if you haven't written for magazines in years, this book is for you. If your writing experience is extremely limited, this book can almost guarantee to jump start your career. I've written this book for you so you can prepare articles in the professional formats editors demand. The only assumption made is that you know the importance of queries, understand the basics of a business letter, can format and write articles and have a workable knowledge of grammar. With that said, you're ready.

Quick and Profitable—The Magazine Writing Game

Want to write articles that sell and sell the articles you write? That's the goal of all of us who make our living from this writing trade. There are ways to do so and it's as easy as counting to four. You must:

1. Make every query marketable and filled with ideas
2. Make sure you know the facts
3. Make your writing sparkle
4. Submit like a professional

In one sentence: Write every article as if you'll forever be known for the material. Strive to be proud of your work. Work at writing and writing (as a profitable profession) will work for you. Some writers think of writing for magazines as a game, not of chance, but with success derived through tenacity, professionalism and staying on top of trends. You can play this game for money or for fun, or if you're like me, you'll do it for both.

Why have you decided to write articles? As you begin to focus on becoming a successful magazine writer, concentrate for a moment on the fact that for almost every article published, an irresistible query letter came first. It's only after the query has been accepted, an agreement arrived at, is the article written. (A query letter is a letter of inquiry written by a writer to an editor "selling" the idea which is then turned into the article. See Chapter 3 for an overview and samples of query letters.)

While queries and good writing play a part in the success of a magazine writer, writers who stop at this point never make it. You can't stop either. You need to know about spin-offs, searching and seizing trends, and discovering "other" markets for your work, including entering the electronic market.

If you're ready to stop dreaming of becoming a magazine writer and want to take the plunge, the good news is that you can do it. There are no wheels to reinvent and no complex schemes to buy into. You just learn the tricks of this trade and get to work. But for the moment, read this book, and then start on your path to a successful career as a magazine writer.

2000 and Beyond—Your Future Starts Today

Think of the magazines you've seen at the supermarket and drugstore. Are you aware that if you only target these publications, you may be missing the sales boat? Barely one-half of one percent of all magazines are sold on the news-stand.

Currently there are over 13,000 magazines published within the United States. Reread that figure—13,000 publications that depend on articles and article ideas from writers like you. No, your local grocery store won't stock them, and the bookstore will probably be of little help to locate scores of these publications. So how can you find magazines, newspapers, newsletters, journals and other periodicals that would consider your work? Go directly to a large public library and ask for: *Newsletters in Print, Ulrich's International Periodicals Directory, Gale Directory of Publications, Standard Periodical Directory, Oxbridge Directory of Newsletters.* (Note: Some libraries may not have them all.)

Ulrich's alone lists over 126,000 periodicals in 554 subject areas. As we move into 2000 and beyond, that figure is predicted to increase. Why? More specialty groups, more specialty publications, more baby boomers (with discretionary income) looking to improve and enhance their lives. These are the same people who want information in a magazine's format.

Right now, there are editors who are looking for articles you will write. If you write well and focus on professionalism, you'll sell even more. Imagine seeing your byline, building credibility, and being paid for your time. It's a dream that can come true.

Producing magazine articles is by far the most lucrative way to break into writing as a living. Yes, and with work, you can quit your day job or devote all your energies to writing. Consider that with over 13,000 magazines and more than 126,000 periodicals published on a regular basis, every publication needs from one to twenty articles each time it goes to press. Even those of us who hated math class can determine that's a sizeable market.

Be realistic

The down side is that novices and hopefuls easily become scattered and fragmented. Beginning writers often think of writing one article and dream of making tens of thousands. Or they don't prepare themselves with the knowledge they need to do a professional writing job. Yet, if you'll focus energy and talent, the odds are increased in any writer's favor.

You don't have to specialize in one field of writing, although many writers find that by concentrating on one topic or field, whether that's writing about pets, peanut butter, or periodontal disease, their reputation is established. Their goal, and possibly yours, is to gain credibility in as many magazines as there's energy and time to pursue and then move into other writing fields.

The thrill of magazine writing is that you can spread your talent around. You could write about foods that help prevent cancer, turbo jet engines, or pigs. The editors at *America*

Baby wouldn't care that you're also an expert on solar-powered airplane engines and write for *Popular Science*. Or that you write newsletter articles for the local YMCA on horsing around with your kids while writing as a contributing editor for *The Equine Image*.

Magazine writers—and that's you—can write for as few or as many publication as they choose. And you can follow your curious nature into other fields. Let's say you want to concentrate on a narrow area, such as senior travel. You can broaden that specialty to include elder care issues, senior discounts, senior investment, nutrition, fitness, and alternative therapies plus cutting-edge insurance coverage. The only limit is your inventiveness.

There are millions of ideas to write about right now and at your finger tips. Every experience you have is material for an article. Have you ever felt amused, frustrated, or afraid waiting in line at the ATM? Do you enjoy quiet Sundays with your kids? Do you collect feathers, car parts, pot holders, door stops? Have you had a psychic experience or a funny experience with someone who believes that she's psychic? Have you ever told a lie? Did you get caught at lying? Do you wonder if tap water is really safe? Have you unearthed your grandmother's recipes and reworked them so that they're lower in fat but not in flavor?

Look again at the paragraph above. Think of what you could write with just these ideas. Some novice writers turn the concept of brainstorming for article topics into a nightmare, but it really is simple. Now imagine them as article titles on the front of your favorite publications. That's how easy it can be to find article ideas. You've done it. You're thinking like a magazine writer. You've already developed some personal slant (that is, the focus) for a magazine. Sure there's more work to be done, but that's how easy it is to make it desirable and salable. Your goal is to write with that focus.

What does it really take to sell to magazines? Good writing, a clean manuscript, care in handling facts and quotes, and the same dedication to deadlines we've needed before. As we move into 2000 and beyond, those requirements will stand.

A degree in English or journalism is fine. It looks nice on a resume, but a bachelor's degree or a doctorate diploma won't help you sell if the query isn't suitable or if you produce an article that isn't suited to a publication.

Your reputation will be enhanced when editors can count on you to provide a professionally prepared article. That has nothing to do with letters after your name. Do not allow a traditional education, or lack of it, to hold you back. "Can do" determination is what counts.

SETTING GOALS AND PRIORITIES

W hat *do* you want to be when you grow up? Being a writer who regularly writes and sells to magazines isn't something that happens along the way to another career. Yet, it can also be a profitable part-time job, sometimes job, or second full-time job.

What does it take to be a magazine writer? Dedication and some say, an obsession for words. Most writers feel the same way I do. Writing is such pleasure that I'd almost do it for free, but I like getting paid better.

In order to succeed at writing or at any profession, one must set goals. There are many excellent books on goal setting and establishing priorities available at the bookstore or library. Get one and use it if you have any desire for success.

A beginner talks about goals, an experienced writer sets them down and accomplishes them. Don't be afraid to set goals and make them tough enough so that you have to work to achieve them. Organize them in any way that works for you—a chart on the wall, a "things-to-do" list, 3 x 5 cards with specific requirements. And as the commercial says, just do it.

THE PROCESS—FROM IDEA TO THE PRINTED PAGE

*E*very magazine article begins with an idea. It's what you *do* with the idea that counts. Let's say you read about the opening of a museum dedicated to the history of the computer. That notice is the spark of an article, but sparks alone don't sell.

The second step is to find out enough about your article idea (the new computer museum) as possible so that you can write an intelligent and interesting query letter. Beginning writers think that they must write the entire article at this point; seasoned writers know they can't waste their time on an article idea that may not sell (even if they adore the idea).

After you have enough information to write the query, you send it to at least ten magazines which normally buy articles on topics similar to yours. For instance with the computer museum idea, *Westways*, *Trailer Life*, Disney's *Family Fun* and *Boy's Life* would be good possibilities. (Note: You still have not written the article and will not do so until you have a firm agreement with a magazine's editor.

When *Westways* responds, then you'll go ahead and write the article. Some articles are written on contract (on assignment) and some on speculation, called "spec." See Chapter 10 for more information on types of contracts.

If your query stated that you'd like to write the article in 1000 words, but *Westways*' editors prefer a shorter version, then you'll agree to this requirement. After writing the article, you send it to the editor along with a query for another topic (may as well while your foot is in the door) and wait.

The lead time or "turn-around time" is the amount of time it takes between your submittal of the article to the actual publication of it, and that depends on the periodical. Some magazines have a lead time (between your submittal and publication) of two months, for others it may be a year. Some editors send the edited, unpublished copy for a writer's review; others don't. If you're unsure of the magazine's policy on this topic, ask.

Then one day it comes. Your mailbox holds a large brown envelope—it's your article. You've done it. You're published. Yet by this time, you've sent queries on other topics to more magazines and have a series of articles on which to work. The life of a magazine writer never stands still. There's always another idea popping up that's too brilliant to dismiss.

Queries

Looking at the writing and sales process, a beginner might say, "I can't bother sending a letter when I've got a great idea now. I'll just bang out an article filled with brilliant words. And besides query letters are hard to write." I've heard this plenty of times in the classes and writing workshops I give.

While there is some logic in this statement (it's fun to bang out articles when the spirit moves you), the logic ends there. Or it should if you're determined to be successful. Why? It could be a gross waste of time to write an article that may not sell. Query letters are cost effective and an efficient use of your valuable time.

Look at the process from the seasoned writer's position. In the beginning, there's a great idea; he or she brainstorms for a unique slant possibly followed by preliminary research, and then writes the query. After receiving an assignment based on the query, the article is written.

This rule does have exceptions, as with fillers, opinion pieces, and short humor, but most of the time, a query comes first.

I write for a living. I don't have the luxury of time to write an article which may not sell. I've been accused of being materialistic, yet the truth is, I have normal, American financial responsibilities. I must sell all the work I write.

Queries are the answer. They take only a fraction of the time to write compared to an article. And queries work yet there's a mystique about them. But there are no secrets where queries are concerned. They all contain the basics. Here's an overview.

The Lead: That's your first paragraph, the hook that will pull in the editor's interest. To work, it must have impact and grab the editor's attention.

How do you do that? Open with an anecdote, provocative quotes, surprising facts, or statistics, references to celebrities or news events, wittiness or exaggeration, references to dramatic events or common situations with a new twist, vivid descriptions, thought-provoking questions, commands to the reader, unusual definitions, and surprising comparisons or contrasts. Your goal is to produce one paragraph that conveys your topic.

For instance, here are a couple leads I've used in queries that sold:

For a family-oriented travel magazine, here's how I began the query about the Computer Museum of America.

> Computer systems used just a few years ago are now obsolete. Quicker than you can say "upgrade," computer technology is being lost. History is being erased nearly as easily as you can hit the key marked "delete."

For a fitness magazine, my query began:

> Riddle time: When is a 10K not a race? A sporting event non-competitive? And everyone from ages 2 to 102 a winner? When it's a volksmarch.

The Second Paragraph: The second paragraph is your summary and you'll want to include what you'll cover and how you'll do it. Here's where you need to have the five "W's": What, where, why, when and who and the "H" for how. Be clear. Use bullets, make points and mention sources and/or experts. List nuts and bolts stuff. Include a working title, if possible. See Chapter 9 for tips on writing titles that can snag an editor's interest.

In this paragraph or the next, give the word length (making sure it matches the length that the magazine uses) and (if appropriate) research or interviews you'll use. You need to sell yourself, too. Why are you the best person possible to write this article? If you don't have a clue, figure out before you send that query. Seriously, here is where you explain that you're so qualified to write this piece that it doesn't matter if you've been published once or a zillion times.

The End: Close it off and move on. "I will be looking forward to hearing from you." Leave the editor on an upbeat note. Include phone number, fax, e-mail address and SASE (a stamped and self-addressed envelope) to make it easy for the editor to get back with you.

If the description of the magazine in one of the guidebooks states that you need to include samples (this can mean unpublished samples) or clips (published samples of your work), then do so.

Remember to write the query in the tone that will be

reflected in your article. If your query is lively and filled with anecdotes, you're probably not going to make a sale if you produce an article that is serious and filled with statistics. Produce the query in the same language style as you plan to write the article.

With queries, success is just a stamp away, yet some writers refuse to make that connection. A well-written query letter is your key to sales. While most writers agree it could be possible make a career as a magazine writer without writing and sending out queries, it's not cost or energy effective.

When teaching and lecturing at writers' conferences and in my university classes, the topic of queries is always a part of the program. New writers are sometimes confused as to when to query. Here's the "basic" rule:

> For short humor, fillers, op-ed, short stories, and some personal viewpoint articles, DO NOT SEND A QUERY. For all the other types of articles, send queries.

Your query must be complete, informative and intriguing. Your goal is to produce the best query you can. If you wait for a stroke of genius, you could be sitting at your desk for weeks. A good query must be interesting and entertaining, factual, pull the editor and reader into what you're saying, and leave the editor and reader satisfied. Regardless of your topic, these points remain constant.

Today's reader wants information fast and fun; note the popularity of *USA Today* and the easy-reading style of *People* and *National Geographic*. Americans, including the well-educated ones, choose to read at a sixth to eighth grade level.

Here are the rules of queries:

•Always keep a copy of your query. You can keep a hard copy or keep it on computer disk, but keep it. You'll be able to recycle that query when the time comes to rewrite the piece or work on spin-offs.

•If plan to get a reply, help the editor. Include your

phone number, fax number, e-mail address and/or send a self-addressed stamped envelope with your query. A SASE will not guarantee you'll get a response, but without it, you've just reduced the odds 50 percent.

•If this is your first query to a magazine and the guidelines request clips of your work, submit your best, most pertinent pieces. If the guidelines request samples and you don't include them, the editor might believe that your credentials are untrue. On the other hand, if you've submitted other queries, a cover letter reflecting that fact that you have previously sent samples. What if you've only written for *Crafts* but want to submit a query to *Verses?* What to do? Send the published samples of your craft projects and articles. These *are* clips and indicate that you can produce articles. It will then be up to your query to convince the editor that your article is right for the magazine. Jot down titles of the photocopied articles sent along with the query. *It goes without saying that if the query is a spin-off or rewritten piece, you would never send the originally published article as an example of your work.*

•Send your writer's resume along with the samples. However, it will not take the place of clips if a magazine specifically requests them.

•Follow through with the article if you get the go-ahead from the magazine editor. Call if you have any questions.

• If your query is turned down—yes, rejected—it's inappropriate to submit the same idea to the same magazine again. Pleading and begging won't work either since there's no exception to this rule.

There are some sample queries that have turned into assigned articles. The basic ideas were turned around to produce additional articles slanted in other directions. Experienced writers know there's more than one way to compose a query and these are presented as samples.

They were produced in a business format and on my letterhead.

Date

Editor's name
Address, etc.

Dear _____:

Keep all correspondence upbeat

Do you know the difference between an ale and a pilsner? Stout and bitter? Even many Americans who prefer fine dining don't. A few of us see beer as the beverage of choice for mechanic types, who spend Sundays with a six-pack discussing the finer points of crankshafts and mufflers.

Beer's come a long way, baby. It's grown up and has attitude. Suddenly it is cool to order a brew. Of course, we're not talking Bud or Coors, but specialty beers from the micro-breweries sprouting up around the country. With the increased interest in micro-breweries and homebrewing, it's time we all knew the history, mythology and basics of beer.

"What's the Brew?" will provide all the information one needs to know on the emergence of specialty beers. The 2000-word article will focus on the hubbub of micro-brews and the why of varieties, tastes, and ingredients used in today's designer beers. It will include a bit of history on brewing, how beer is brewed commercially (and why most brewing virtuosos will suffer from a parched throat rather than drink a *can* of beer), and a scoreboard of beer types (along with how the tastes differ).

The article will include interviews with homebrewers and micro-brewery owners such as those from Voluptuous Blond Ale, Saxer Lemon, and Rattlesnake Brew. And it will attempt to predict the future of beer. I'll also include a small sidebar on Web Pages and magazines devoted to the hobby of brewing.

As part of an amateur brewing family and a beer-tasting snob (or so I've been called since I have a refined sense of taste), I am also the author of *Writing and Selling Magazine Articles* and many other books and magazine articles. I teach writing at the University of California, through private college programs, and at workshops throughout the country. I'd very much like to submit this article and hope you'll consider it.

Thanks for your attention.

Sincerely,

Eva Shaw, Ph.D.
Enclosure

Date

Editor's name
Address, etc.

Dear _____:

I'd like to submit a 1200-word article called "Learning to Live Alone." Based on my counseling work and my award-winning book *What to Do When a Loved One Dies* (resume and review are enclosed), it will be a positive, useful feature and one everyone needs to read.

"Alone" doesn't mean lonely; rather it means one has become separate from others. There may be many alone times in our lives, many because of our own choices. The article will include why we are alone such as after the end of a relationship, end of a career, or the separation caused from death, or family changes. It will examine our "alone feelings," such as depression, obsessions, further removal from society. It will give help with ways of discovering inner peace, letting go of fears of loneliness, and finding strength in seclusion.

I'll explain ways to change loneliness to the joy of living alone, such as making one's presence felt, learning to relax and taking care of one's own needs, stopping lonely behaviors, seeking knowledge, touching and reconnecting, and most importantly, ways to reinvent oneself.

Eleanor Roosevelt said, "You must do the thing you think you cannot do." Sometimes that even means learning to live alone.

Please consider this topic, and thank you for your consideration.

Sincerely,

Eva Shaw, Ph.D.
PS: If you'd like a copy of the book (recently seen with me on MSNBC, The Maury Povich Show, The Leeza Show and mentioned once again in *Newsweek*, and the basis for a MetLife "Life Advice" brochure, let me know and I'll ask my publisher to send you a copy.

Querying and Getting a Response

Just because you get a SASE (self-addressed, stamped envelope) in the mail, it doesn't mean a rejection; a self-addressed stamped envelope is used as a convenience for the editor of the magazine to contact you. As a skilled writer, most of the time that SASE brings great news: an assignment, a contract, or a lead to some other article topic that's even better than the one queried.

Traditionally, when a writer sends a query, he or she includes a SASE. These days, it's not necessary to tell an editor that you're including one. It's assumed that you have.

I keep a prepared supply of SASE's to make it more time efficient when churning out query letters. The format's on my computer's hard drive. In addition to having my return address typed and centered in the middle of the SASE, I place the name of the magazine just below my return address in the top left hand corner. When I open the mailbox and see one of my printed envelopes, I like to know immediately which magazine is writing.

I send SASE's with queries to magazines that prefer the

practice *or* if there's something I want returned. However, because information is now easily available for reproduction from computer disks, many writers have gone to a quicker method. They use a SASP—self-addressed stamped post-card, mass produced with their software or at the copy shop. The front of the card has the writer's name and address and the return address of the magazine to which the query has been sent. The back had the title of the query plus notations such as:

Query title: (filled in by writer)

Date received:

Dear Editor: Thank you for your consideration. I know your time is limited. Please let me know your response by checking the appropriate line.

_____   Yes, send the article, contract follows.

_____   Yes, please call me for details.

_____   No thanks. Call me for another slant/idea/topic.

_____   Can't use this topic because_____.

Editor's name _____

Using a SASE, expect to be patient from weeks to a few months. Those who use SASPs report response time is reduced.

Be aware that some experienced magazine writers do not use SASEs or SASPs. They say it's not necessary since they're professionals. I still use them because, I think, anything that makes an editor's life easier so he or she will look more favor-ably on my query is worth a stamp.

Unless a foreign publication specifically requests interna-tional reply coupons (IRC's), it's unnecessary to send them. Sending United States stamps is useless. Depending on the foreign publication, and whether I've worked with them before, I include a prepared self-addressed envelope submitted along with my query. Having that addressed envelope often speeds a positive reply.

One more word about SASEs, be sure to include enough postage. If you are sending a query letter, a few samples of your work and a SASE, you may be over the one ounce limit. Having to find another stamp in order to return your query will slow the process even more for a harried editor.

Is it ever appropriate to query by phone? As you regularly work with a magazine's editor, you'll know whether he or she likes article ideas over the phone. If it's okay, ask for a few minutes to pitch an article. Tell enough to get the assignment and to capture the editor's interest.

With editors and magazines you haven't worked with before, telephone queries are tricky. Some accept telephone queries. Others won't bother with you until they review clips of your work.

Telephone queries do require organization. Write out the query, think of the answer to possible questions, and have all the information in front of you before you make that call. Be prepared to wait or to repeat your query to an assistant before talking with the editor. If necessary, leave your query on his or her voice mail, and repeat your phone number and name twice.

Telephone queries are advisable when your topic is an exclusive, a new item, or extraordinary. But again be organized with all the information *before* you call or you won't be able to sell the editor no matter how brilliant your query is.

The Query Blitz

There was a time when students of "Magazine Writing 101" were told they must only submit a query to one magazine at a time. The teacher and even some editors inferred that it was immoral to do otherwise; i.e., use the multiple submission method. Beginners continue to practice this antiquated system.

In the real world, query letters get lost, are ignored, are put at the bottom of a stack of incoming mail from editors who don't have time to reply because they are overworked. If you use the one-at-a-time system, be prepared to wait for a response.

Keep your approach professional

As a determined magazine writer, feel free to utilize the "blitz" method of sending out queries. This method works extremely well. You can computer merge a pre-determined list of magazine addresses with the body of the query letter. It works just as well if you must individually type each letter. However, don't be tempted to run down to your local copy store to photocopy your query. That's tacky.

The blitz system works quite easily and will continue to work well into the next century. From your research, *Writer's Market, Literary Market Place, The Writer* or other listings of publications, select seven to ten magazines which routinely buy the type of article explained in your query. Send each a query letter, along with a SASE or SASP. Keep a list of the magazines and a copy of your query. As soon as a magazine editor writes or calls with an okay, and you agree to the terms of the contract, start writing the article.

What happens if two magazine editors say yes? Choose the magazine that will do the most for your career, has the most potential for additional sales or, of course, offers the most money. But what should you do with the second or third positive reply? Be honest. Write or call the editor, explain that you've just spoken to another editor and the idea was snapped up. However, you happen to have another sterling topic. Then explain it. *Or* write or call the editor and offer the same topic with another irresistible slant.

I maintain a separate query file on each topic, such as one for "Water" for the example above. Not every query represents a sale; this is real life. I don't make up a file for a particular magazine until I've made a sale. When that happens, I place query, response, article, and further correspondence into a file. Those queries which are out to "new" magazines (one's I haven't sold to before) are stored (on my computer— but you can use paper, too) in a document file marked "Queries."

In the query file, I keep a mailing list of the magazines, a copy of a specific query, the magazines I sent the query to, and the date and the response. This method helps when going back to resell or change the slant of a query so I can sell a spin-off. I only stop sending that query when I'm no longer anxious to write the article or the topic is out-of-date.

Initially, it might be difficult to come up with other topics when an editor calls. This temporarily confuses newcomers. Experienced writers keep that list of slants (developed during the original brainstorming session) in the query file, pull it up on the screen and pitch the idea. You can also politely ask if you can call the editor back in ten minutes, hunt through the query file or get creative right then.

Let's say, an editor for *Sailing* calls and wants more information on an article you queried three months before. You've already sold the article to *Key West Sail Newsletter*, and it's to be published in a few weeks. Be honest. "Thanks for calling; however, since I didn't hear from your magazine, I sold the article to another magazine. How about an article on (add in the topics)."

Amateur writers are surprisingly terrorized by the thought of talking with an editor. They'd never think or dare to go the extra mile or attempt to sell an editor on an alternative topic. Veteran writers know that editors need articles, need good writers, and appreciate ideas. Be polite, but don't be shy.

Just one-a-day is all it takes to set you apart from beginning writers and to sell your work. I use and highly recommend the one-a-day sure-proof sales program. It's simple. It works. Make your goal to send one query a day, minimum.

Regarding queries, I average one a day over a month's time. That means, sometimes I send out ten in one day and then go for a while without submitting queries. During really busy periods, I often begin the day with that one query (kept on my hard drive or on disk) then get back to the assigned article I'm writing.

Is it appropriate to call or write to check on a query? If so, when should you do it? Those are two of the most often asked questions in my magazine article writing classes.

Since I recommend and use the blitz method, I normally write the article for the first magazine that contacts me in response to my query. Until the time I sell an article from the query, I always keep from seven to ten queries circulating to magazine editors.

Wait about two weeks before calling. Have all the information in front of you (and even written out if you think you might forget something—that's what I do on complex subjects). Mail and queries get lost and your phone call might be the first time an editor has heard of you or the topic. Be prepared to soft sell over the phone should this be the case.

What should you say? After a courteous and business-like opening mentioning your name and the fact that you're the freelancer who sent _____ (add working title of query), briefly explain: "I submitted a query on (add the topic) about two weeks ago, and I'm calling to find out if a decision has been made?" Let your smile and enthusiasm be transmitted in that call. Make the call effective.

When you telephone, be prepared for a rejection. You don't really know what's happening in the editor's office or life and why the rejection has occurred. He or she may have been in a fender-bender accident on the way to work, may be ill, may have just had an argument with a co-worker or spouse. Don't take rejection personally.

You might not get a simple yes or even a rejection. Be prepared if the editor asks for an extension of time to consider the query. If you're encouraged to submit other queries, don't trust your memory. Scribble down what the editor has in mind and then submit queries on these topics, if you like the ideas, as soon as possible. State in your letter that the editor suggested you write. While on the phone, ask for the correct spelling of the editor's name. Some experienced writers mark the envelope with: "Query Requested." They think it speeds the process.

If you have a rapport with the editor, take notes about the personal things he or she talks about, including staff, hobbies, kids, favorite movies, or authors the editor enjoys. For example let's say an editor comments, "It's a crazy day. I'm babysitting a friend's frisky Welsh Terrier and the dog demands a four-mile sunrise walk each morning at six and I can barely get the kids out of the house by 7:30." The next time you call, you might ask if the pooch got home okay. Did everyone survive the visit?

Sound as though you're buttering up the editor? What really happens is that the editor knows you see him or her as more than just a means to being published in the magazine. Your goal is to allow your personality to come through. You are a real person, not just a writer.

If your conversation is pleasant, the editor will remember you. Here again, pick up clues whether or not the editor has time for small talk. If not, don't be offended and just get right back onto the topic at hand.

If you choose to write a letter as a follow-up to a query, be business-like, include the working title of your proposed article and briefly cover your sales pitch. Once more, this may be the first time the editor has seen anything from you. Enclose a SASE or a stamped postcard along with your follow-up letter.

A Query or the Entire Article?

We'll go into how to write queries to sell articles in detail later in the book. For now, let's talk about cost efficiency, the effective use of your time.

What if that article doesn't sell? Then you'd feel frustrated. What if you wrote a query and had it refused? Sure you might feel frustrated, but you'll know right off if the topic you're proposing is marketable and then can make a decision as to how much time you'll spend writing the article.

Writing a query could take you a few hours; writing an article could take you a few days or even a few weeks. Queries are cost effective. They make sense.

With the choices, the bottomline doesn't change because at once you'll ask, when does the publication pay me? Because writing is my living that's on my mind often. And, depending on the publication, the answer varies. There are magazines that pay on receipt of your article. Others send the check when the issue hits the newsstand or goes out to subscribers. A few pay up to three months after publication. A lesser number require you to hound them for the funds.

Check writer's guidelines obtained from magazines or the information in the listings in *The Writer* and *Writer's Digest*. Notice that some magazines pay on acceptance and others pay on publication. "On acceptance" means they'll pay when the article is accepted for publication. Of course, that may or may not mean when the editor says, "Hey, I love it." The time may actually stretch to when the magazine goes to press.

"On publication" translates to when the magazine is out on the newsstand or sent to subscribers. Some writers will not work with publications that pay this way. Why? They're concerned that they'll have to wait forever to be paid.

Like most freelance writers, you'll have to face the decision of writing for magazines which pay on acceptance or on publication with other benefits. What's the exposure for your name or material? Do you want to get into a new periodical? Will writing the article link you with other publications in the same genre?

Just because a magazine editor says the publication pays on publication, it doesn't mean that's the way they pay all writers. After writing a few articles, talk with the editor. If you're good and the policy is flexible, you may be able to alter the situation.

Timing Your Submittal/Query

When should you send a query on a trend, seasonal piece, or timely news article? Most novices check *Writer's Digest* or *The Writer*, look at the writer's guidelines, see that seasonal material is accepted six months in advance, and send a query or submits the article.

The accomplished magazine writer knows that six months is the deadline—that's probably the date the presses roll. He or she gets the query to the editor eight or nine months ahead of that time. Why? Let's look at the system. It takes about a week for your query to reach the proper editor's desk, a few days to come to the top of the basket, at least another day to be processed and have him or her say, "Yes, that's a great idea—go ahead. Enclosed is our writer's contract," etc. Now add a few more days for your response to make it to the mail room to be processed by the postal system. Then it's back to you for you to research and write the article. If you wait until seasonal deadline to submit a query, you'll have missed the boat and the assignment.

As freelancers learn quickly, never write just one article on a topic. Changing the slant is where the profits come. If you have a really hot idea that's been mulling around in your head, go directly to the section on writing irresistible queries and get your queries in the mail *today*.

Experienced magazine writers know that if they think an article topic is worthy of being published, there's another writer out there who is also attuned to the same thought pattern. When lecturing on this *Act on your ideas!* topic, I talk about the Wright Brothers. They're known as the inventors of the airplane, and we hardly ever consider those other brave souls who, if they were lucky, ended up with only bruised egos because they didn't get the word out to the media that they were flying, too.

In my "other job" as a ghostwriter, I wrote a book for a woman in the networking and advertising business. I knew writers could profit from networking tips, but I'm guilty because it took me six months to send a query on networking to *Writer's Digest*. Yesterday's mail brought the rejection—the editor scribbled across my query, "Sorry, Eva. Already have another piece on similar subject."

Want to "fly"? Then move with that query when an idea strikes, or like magic, someone else will write it. This has nothing to do with being unethical or immoral. Your query must reach an editor before the other freelance writer's query does.

With news, trends, holiday or seasonal pieces, or any other topics, don't wait. Format an irresistible query letter and get it out to the specific magazine buying that type of article. Remember the Wright Brothers—

The Format You Need to Succeed

Beginning writers somehow have the misconception that they can be creative in article submission format. Not true. By submitting a manuscript that's produced in a "creative" format, odds are that it will be rejected without being read. Here's how to avoid that possibility.

•All manuscripts should be typed and double spaced, with between 210 and 240 words per page (except the first and last page). Do not place extra lines between paragraphs. Indent paragraphs five spaces.

•Set margins at 1 inch on each side, including the top and bottom of the page. Do not justify the right margin (this can throw the word count off, and editors do not like full justification). On second and subsequent pages, begin text 1 inch from the top of the sheet. On the first page, center the title about 5 inches from the top.

•Your name, address, phone number, e-mail address, and social security number should appear on the first page in the top left corner. Do not double space this information. In the left corner indicate the approximate word count. On the second and following pages, type your name and the "slug," a shortened version of the title, in the top left corner. Number all pages.

•Select a font that is dark and easy to read. For example San serif, Courier and Roman are suitable in a 10 cpi (characters per inch), 12 point font. Italic, extra-fancy and oversize fonts are not appropriate for manuscripts and may lead to rejection of even dazzling work.

•Your goal is to produce assignments that are within 10 percent (plus or minus) of the required word count. Providing a correct word count of an article is a mark of a professional.

(Note: For tips on naming your "baby" [that is, titling the article] see Chapter 9.)

How Are Articles Assigned?

After you send a query to the magazine's editor, you'll be contacted with the assignment. The editor should talk about the money issue too, and if money isn't discussed, bring it up. If you're shy, you may go without pay.

You're a professional and this is your job. I like to ask: "What's your budget for this type of article?" Or: "What are the normal rates for articles this length?" If the amount offered isn't enough, say so. Tell the editor your current rate.

Sometimes and in some places, we simply need to write an article and money isn't the true propelling force. If that's true, figure that in your equation. Also consider a publication's distribution. Would you take less to have your article and byline into the hands of 20 million readers? Find out about copyrights—can you resell a piece? Is the topic so timely that you'll only have one chance to sell it, then less might be more again.

Go with the flow of the assignment. If what is being offered is too little, say you're not interested. There will be more assignments and more work. Look at the big picture of your career and where you've been already. Then get back to work and send out more queries.

A Writer's Resume

Experienced writers often shy away from writing a resume. I think of it as a time-saving device. Once it's on the hard drive of my computer, it's easy to print and send with query letters or include in the query.

There are two important reasons for writing a resume—it forces you to list the articles you've written (or in your corporate life, the types of material you've created) and the magazines in which you've been published. It boosts your ego to see you are a working writer.

What should you list? Some writers include everything. Some only include a few of the top or most well-known publications. You may want to have a few different styles of resume available, such as one listing books and magazines and another with newspaper credits.

With over one thousand published magazine credits, I often change my resume. For example if I were querying a gardening magazine, I would make sure my resume included that I have been published in outdoor and related publications, such as *Garden Design* and *Garden and Home Guide*. For an educational publication, such as *Instructor*, I'd stress that I teach through the Extension Branch of the University of California and have been published in various teaching magazines.

In addition to a resume, I have a "creative" resume available. Rather than list the magazine and books I've written, the bio tells about Eva Shaw, the writer and specifics about my style and success. Some writers have a home page telling about their background and experience and provide their website address on their stationary or resume.

Like a resume for a job, your resume or bio should include all that is professional and delete personal stuff (height, shoe size, sex, religious connection, breakfast cereal preference, etc.). Do include your e-mail address or fax number if you have one and your educational background if appropriate.

Try to keep your resume to one page, and photocopy or print it on white or a neutral-colored paper. Double check for typos. It's a reflection of your professionalism.

A Confirmation Letter

The best has happened: An editor called about your query. "Hey, we love it," he said while you silently jumped for joy. Then he added, "Go ahead and send it in."

After you exhale and dance around the room, go directly to your word processor and confirm the assignment's verbal agreement. Do this immediately. Why? The letter reiterates exactly what you're expected to do and what you expect from the magazine.

Here's a sample confirmation letter:

Date
Editor's Name
Address, etc.

Dear _____:

Thank you for calling and giving approval for me to submit _____ (fill in your article's title).
As we discussed, the article will be approximately _____
(fill in word count). The due date for the article is _____
(fill in date). I will submit the names, addresses and phone numbers of all those I interview.
I understand that the article is written on contract and payment of (fill in the amount) is due on acceptance.
Enclosed is an article idea in which I thought you might be interested.
Sincerely,

Don't make it complex but confirm the terms of your conversation or letter with:

- Working title
- Length
- Photos or illustrations, if applicable
- Deadline
- Payment
- The copyrights you are selling
- Whether this is a confirmed assignment or to be written on spec
- Social security number

Some writers ask the editor to sign the confirmation letter and return a copy. I've never found that necessary on magazine articles, but it's a personal decision that you as an experienced writer must make. Definitely keep a copy of your letter for your own files.

Letters of confirmation are essential when accepting telephone assignments—so get it in writing. If a point wasn't clear or the editor didn't convey the information, your letter will jog the editor's memory and you'll confirm the terms of the assignment without any catch.

Four 4

HOW SUCCESSFUL WRITERS READ MAGAZINES

*T*hose with little experience in writing get so tied up with methods to bulletproof their submittals that they forget they have to get those queries out to get assignments. Analyzing magazines and their needs is simple.

In a perfect world you'd review a magazine and plenty of its back issues before you sent a query. I can hear your writing teacher telling you so. Although I teach writing, this is one golden rule I've *never* accepted because sometimes you simply cannot get a copy of the publication.

Should that stop you from sending a query? Absolutely not. Even the really big city libraries have just a tiny margin of the thousands of publications found in the marketplace. If you do have access to magazines, that's wonderful. If you don't, query anyhow because there may be times when even reviewing one issue of a magazine is impossible.

How so? It might be a new magazine or a trade publication. It could be a regional publication. It could be a limited edition magazine. Novice writers will not query because they think it's futile to write a query letter without a copy.

Make no mistake, it's not the easiest way, but it *is* possible. Recently, I received an advertisement about a new magazine just for people who enjoy visiting health resorts. I have written for the fitness market and done spa-oriented articles for years. I knew the topic and the lingo. The magazine's ad said it would start publication in the fall and it listed names of forthcoming articles. No, there was no editorial office listed in the advertisement, so I tracked down the address of the head office through their distribution center. I wanted to query this magazine.

After locating the office address, I called and got the editor's name. She wasn't in, but I had enough to start. I wrote a query about "Spa-ing in Finland." As we go to press with this book, the editor is editing my article. All from an advertisement for a magazine that hasn't been published yet. Remember, if I can do this, so can you.

Of course there are easier ways. Read about the magazine's wants and needs, such as found in various periodical listings, then follow the description carefully. For instance, if the magazine uses only interview articles with landscape experts, or articles about products strictly for libraries, a how-to piece about North African cooking or an interview with Sting is going to be rejected pretty quick.

This gives you a contact to reference

The secret's in the masthead. Inside the first few pages of any publication is a listing of the employees who produce the magazine along with their job titles. This is the masthead. Look at this area closely.

If the magazine you're analyzing is small, like *Feedlot Magazine*, it might only have an editor/publisher, production editor, art director, a writer, subscription director, and account (advertising) director.

Large publications, such as *Time*, have a masthead that lists a variety of editors and creative personnel.

Your job is to be able to translate this information to help you sell articles. Why? You want to direct your query to the right individual or it may forever be placed in a black hole and lost. So when there's a choice of editors, as with the example above, send queries to the most appropriate individual on the masthead.

Keep in mind that "editor" does not necessarily mean this individual reads queries and assigns articles. A few years back, I worked with a trade magazine for the beauty and barbering industry. It was a small publication (about 10,000 subscribers). The editor-in-chief served as the real editor, i.e., he edited the copy for the magazine. The production editor worked with layout and the design crew. And you've probably guessed, I wrote all the copy that went through this process.

In large publications, a publisher or editor-in-chief rarely works with writers; she or he is in charge of the magazine's administration. A managing editor might work with writers or might not. A feature editor might really only write copy and not edit others' work. A production editor could, like at "my" trade magazine, be responsible for production of the magazine page, cover, and any other ads or copy.

That said and confusion understood, what does a writer do? Look for titles such as editor, articles editor or a specific editor (such as features editor, parenting editor, landscape editor) for clues.

Then contact the magazine by phone and double check your guessing ability. You can speak with the receptionist and get even more information, but make note, it's wise to know what you're going to say before you dial the phone. While it's your  dime, find out the spelling of the editor's name. We all appreciate having our name spelled correctly.

So what if you don't take this time to figure out the real editor to query? If you're lucky, your query will eventually land on the appropriate editor's desk. If you're not, it will be lost. Reduce the odds of the second happening by targeting the most appropriate editor. You'll help an editor make a decision on your material in the shortest amount of time. If that magazine editor passes on your query, you can send it to another.

WHERE DO PROFITABLE IDEAS COME FROM?

"The Bubble Method" (also known as clustering and mind mapping) is a powerful technique writers use to brainstorm and to outline articles and queries. (Magazine writers who also write fiction use this method to develop plots, characters, and message.)

Bubble Power for Outlining Success

For the Bubble Method, print the topic of your article in the middle of a blank piece of paper, draw a circle around it and then add ten lines out from the circle, or bubble. You have what looks like a child's drawing of the sun with a word in the center. Without censoring your thoughts, write ten subtopics that are somehow related to your main topic. Circle them, too. That's it. Simple and powerful.

What you may find when "bubbling" is that you like one

or more of the subtopics better than the original one. You guessed it—that's the one to further research and query. Start with another piece of paper and place your subtopic "bubble" in the middle, and then "bubble" off again. Each of the ten sub-subtopics can now be turned into main ideas for each paragraph of your article.

You can go back and outline the way we all learned in school, but try the bubble method for the sheer creativity of it.

Cashing In on Your Experience

As I always tell my writing students and remind myself quite often, write from experience. Write about what *you* know. And if you follow this practice, you'll sell what you write.

If you're over the age of eight, you're an expert on something. Should you ever run out of topics to query for your "one a day" query letter program, or if you are looking for material, start right in your own head with personal experiences, hobbies, relationships, careers, goals and dreams.

This does not mean opinion pieces or personal essays (unless that's an area in which you're interested). It means you'll already be familiar with the topic which places you a step ahead of the competition. I love to do craft projects. A few years back *Sunset* magazine published one of my ideas (and photographed me) in a multi-page spread. I turned a "hobby" into something marketable and you can do it too.

And then you can become an expert on something new. We sometimes hear: Follow your passions. If you're interested in a topic, learn about it. Then take it a step further and figure out how you can write about it.

Using Proven Fiction Techniques for Articles

Few magazine articles have beautiful damsels with quivering rosebud lips and swashbuckling heros ready to leap tall buildings for their lady love. However, as magazine writers, we must use some fiction techniques to create powerful, compelling, passionate language. A bored reader equates to a bored editor—and that means no sale.

Next time you're reading fiction, see how your favorite author keeps you glued to that page. Is it the tempo of the words, the variations in sentence length, the dialogue (for us that would be expert quotes), or  the comparisons. Are colors brighter through the eyes of Zora Neale Hurston, eyes more sparkling when described by Danielle Steele, heroes more shrewd when Tom Clancy writes about them? Stop envying the words that fiction writers use, and start using them. You could write: The sky was blue. Or you could hit the thesaurus and come up with dozens of variations. Don't forget similes and metaphors, humor, drama. For goodness' sake, Hallmark and Kodak keep selling to us because our emotions get involved.

If you feel as if you've lost your fresh edge, review fiction books on building strong characters, setting scenes, developing plots.

The All-Important Interview

An interview? It's nothing more than talking and getting information. It's a variation on a conversation. An interview is required to provide information for writing articles. Interviews are needed to get the facts or an account of events. Interviews provide the basis of popular writing.

Some writers quake at the thought of interviewing. They avoid the prospect of interviewing an expert, and the interview looms over the article they want to write. They avoid it and sideline career opportunities.

Whether you're planning an article on how to collect baseball cards or how to stop card room gambling, an interview with an expert livens it up like nothing else. That interview adds essential, colorful anecdotes to substantiate the article's information. Interviews are woven into all of the most popular types of articles, especially the how-to articles. They also double your prospects for a sale.

Interviews are the basis for personality profiles. Celebrities, scientists, the rich, high-tech gurus, intriguing folks and the newsmakers are continually featured in profiles that are the backbone of many popular magazines including *US* and *People* and the trade journals, such as *Shopping Center World* and *Business NH Magazine*. As you network with experts and interesting people, always think about cross-markets and how you can rewrite the same article giving it a whole new incarnation.

By now you've probably done interviews, but the person you're interviewing may never have talked with a real live writer. Or it may be a first interview for both of you. Your job is to make that individual feel comfortable and better able to communicate. Why? You'll get a better interview when your expert is relaxed.

Here are some ice-breaking questions:

Always use open-ended questions. Avoid "yes" or "no" questions.

- What do you most appreciate about your life?
- What was your greatest ambition when you started?
- What was the best/toughest time in your life?
- What is the biggest disappointment you've had?
- What do you like most/least about yourself?
- What are you most proud of?

When using quotes, provide the correct punctuation so that your reader knows who is saying what. If you're unsure about the rules of dialogue, get a book from the library or study and duplicate the punctuation used in the magazine you'll be writing for.

You don't have to love interviewing, but you have to learn how to do it—think of it as a college class that's required to get your degree. If you intend to write for magazines, you will be interviewing—no two ways about it.

Before you arrange an interview, research the topic you plan to write about. Find out as much as you can about the topic under discussion and the expert who is graciously giving you that interview. If you fail to do so, the expert you're interviewing will know. He or she will also not give you a good interview.

Let's say a lucky novice writer wangles an interview with the head of a large corporation. The CEO personally supports inner city theater with time and money. If the first question is: "So, Mrs. Jones, where did you get that delightful accent?" Sounds like a safe question, but our novice just blew it.

Cordial as she might be, Mrs. Jones is going to know immediately that the novice didn't bother to find out that she grew up in a tough part of Birmingham, Alabama. Now Mrs. Jones is wondering *what else* the novice didn't bother to find out. It's doubtful that the writer is going to score any points or get any insider's information by such an obvious lack of preparation.

When you research and learn about your expert or the expert's topic, you honor the individual. It's flattering to know that the expert you're interviewing was a Rhodes scholar, has had poetry published, and had dropped out of high school only to become your town's most influential citizen.

Here are some interview how-tos to make the next one easier.

• Since most articles benefit by an expert's opinion, make it part of your research to locate someone who is an authority. This does not mean that the individual you hope to interview has a doctorate, just that the person knows more about the topic than others. He or she may be an eye witness to a disaster, the inventor of a new birdhouse, or the local police chief.

• Then contact the person (or people). Explain you're planning an article and the topic of the interview. Keep notes—what the expert says in the preliminary interview can make for intriguing questions when you're face to face.

• Ask a few questions indicating you know something about the person or topic. Ask if you may have a half-hour for the interview. (Be prepared to do the interview then, over the phone, but most likely, your expert will want to schedule it for another time.) Find out when it is convenient to call or come to the expert's office. Confirm the interview.

• If the interview is premature (that is, you don't have a definite assignment yet), you might say, "As soon as the magazine I've contacted replies, we'll set a time for the interview." You might ask what materials (books, newspaper reports, etc.) the expert recommends that you read before the interview. This can provide more information and more experts to interview.

• Be friendly; your voice should give a warm, first impression. Leave a phone number. If you strike out contacting an expert, don't be alarmed; ask if this person knows someone else in the field with whom you might talk.

• Check your "equipment" before the interview. Do you have fresh batteries in your tape recorder? Do your pens work? Do you have a tissue should a sneeze erupt? Do you know where you're going and have an alternate route should the highway be under construction? Do you have change for a phone call (if you're running late), the parking meter, or valet?

• For the interview, dress like a professional magazine writer. Even if it's not fair, we are judged on our appearance, yet a suit isn't always appropriate. If I'm interviewing a race-horse breeder at her stable in Kentucky, I'll wear a sporty casual outfit. Switch that interview to a Montana horse ranch 100 miles from where the road ends, and jeans, t-shirt, boots and jacket or blazer make more sense.

• Be prepared with questions and write them out. If it's

good enough for top network journalists, it's fine for us working writers. I take notes and tape interviews. Some writers transcribe the interview immediately (often stopping for coffee on the way back to the office), and others wait until the quotes are needed in the article. Do what works for you.

• During the interview, keep cross-marketing at the forefront of your thoughts. Spin-offs make experienced writers richer.

When I worked with a fitness magazine, my job was to interview celebrities. One of the stars was Lou Ferrigno (star of the old television series "The Incredible Hulk"). What an opportunity and what a nice person. The moment I met him I knew right off to turn one interview into much more. And that's what I did. That one interview was material for the fitness magazine, and then I put a new spin on it for a body building magazine. Stop there? No way. I looked at my notes and listened to the tapes again and turned out a food article, (we had talked about his favorite omelette recipe and he offered a photo of himself and his wife in the kitchen). I also wrote a short piece for a parenting magazine about the needs of children of celebrity parents. Now that's time well spent, but it didn't stop there.

Meeting his vivacious wife, Carla, during the interview, I contacted her later. During our initial small talk, I found out that at one time, she'd been quite heavy—I wrote an article for *Weight Watcher's Magazine* on her exercise tips. All that from a thirty minute conversation. You can do it, too, especially if you research your expert well in advance and get into a mind-set that you *can* sell spin-offs.

• Depending on the topic, you may need to have the individual sign a letter or form stating that you have an exclusive on the interview. You may also need a photo release if there are photographs of the person included in your article.

• Follow through with what you say you'll do and that includes sending the individual you've interviewed a copy of the published article. Some writers allow the person they've interviewed to read the article, other's refuse. You must make that an individual decision with each interview or find out about the policy of the magazine.

• During the interview, remind yourself that you're there to listen. It is *so* difficult at times not to stop and chat with the interesting people you'll interview. However, if you do that, you won't have all your questions answered and the time will have been wasted.

• Stay "connected" with the expert using appropriate body language. Scowling, with arms crossed over your chest, will not help you get a great interview. Rather show you're pleased, happy, honored, gratified, etc. to be there for the interview. This person *is* helping you achieve further career success.

• Always wind down near the end of the interview, and then ask *the* most important question (which can only be asked at the end of the interview): Is there anything you'd like to add or other topics you'd like to talk about that we haven't covered?

Your expert may have been patiently waiting for the last half hour to tell you something so crucial it will make your article. If you don't ask this important question, you'll never know.

• Before you leave, make sure that the expert has your business card. You might say, "In case you need to reach me or if there's something you want to add to the interview, here's my card." What if he or she remembers something that's usable for the article but has no way to reach you—well, you get the point.

• When you return to your office, send the expert a quick note of thanks. Few people actually take pen to paper these days, and your courtesy will be remembered. Besides, you'll never know when you'll need to reach this expert again—or vice versa.

Telephone, Translated and Special Interviews

As technology advances, more interviews will be done over the phone and via e-mail. While telephone interviewing is not the first choice for most writers, time and travel constraints make it more cost effective. With an interview conducted using e-mail, you'll simply send your questions and expect the reply. Using an e-mail list, Usenet newsgroup, or IRC Chat, ask your expert a question. Then you'll get the reply before following up with another question.

How do you transcribe the interview? You can jot notes or work up the interview right in the article. For a lengthy or technical interview, it may need to be transcribed verbatim. And then you may be the kind of writer, like myself, who prefers to tape telephone interviews, jotting notes afterward, and listening to the interview again when I'm ready to use it.

It's good manners to formally advise the person you're interviewing that he or she is being interviewed. Also that you're taping the interview (and it's the law in a few states, including here in California). If you have a number of interviews to do for one article, mark the tapes, or put them into separate envelopes marked with pertinent information such as the name, date and phone number of the person interviewed. I staple the envelope closed and attach it to a copy of the signed interview release form.

There may be times when you'll interview individuals who speak limited English or are hearing-impaired, and you'll be doing the interview with the help of a translator. Make sure the individual who is being interviewed and the translator both know you'll be using the translator's words as they are spoken. Address the individual when you're talking. Give the translator plenty of time, look at the expert as what you've said is translated, and double check any items you're unsure of. Allow extra time. Translated interviews take longer than you expect.

Special interviews also include three-way or group conversations. As you tape the interview or record notes, be sure to indicate with an initial or code which person is speaking.

As you interview, include your thoughts jotted in the margin of your note pad. You may not remember the color of his or her eyes, what the office view looked like, or even the fragrance he or she was wearing when you transcribe the notes. Including the observation of emotions and the senses into an article, as you know, makes it come alive for the reader.

Sidebars and the Interview

Sidebars, small supporting articles that are included with an article, are an important part of today's article. As you begin to think about and use the cross-market, spin-offs and reuse of material, keep the quotes and interviews.

As you interview, think of how one portion of the interview could be turned into a sidebar. Pretend you've just interviewed an award-winning actor/director on the future of funding for stage productions. A sidebar might contain quotes about a high school play, a first acting coach, the performance the actor remembers best. Sidebars must add to the article.

A Million Slants

The "slant" for the query and subsequent article is the main theme. It must be evident in your irresistible query letter. It must be unmistakable in your article. Let's look at your topic from an unorthodox perspective. Remember, nobody is going to make fun of your creative musings unless you let them. So I hereby give you permission to go absolutely crazy with all the unconventional slants for any article you want to write and sell.

Turn on your creative juices. Brainstorm. Suppose you see a requirement in a certain publication for an article on volunteerism. Most magazines that sell to the public would buy a good piece on this topic—if it has a twist. If you wanted to, you could go off to your computer, work a while and get those queries in the mail on volunteer opportunities. That's the beginner's process.

Sit quietly for a moment and think up a new twist. How can you approach the topic to catch an editor's jaded eye and sell an article? Try these suggestions for starters:

•Outlandish volunteering opportunities—rescuing tadpoles from a swamp that's infested with bugs.

•Interviewing a local single parent who coaches a Special Olympics swimming team.

•Talking to those involved in Habitat for America, or people who are restoring part of Ellis Island (the New Jersey side).

•A day in the life of a volunteer at a free clinic, someone who flies medical supplies to Third World nations, a pet rescue team.

As you brainstorm, scribble all your ideas, even the silly ones. Don't censor yourself, and if you're tempted to stop without a concept that sounds really marketable, it's too soon. It's the fourth, fifth and sixth slant that makes money. You might find that you can create many articles out of one topic.

Let's consider an article on the benefits of gardening. Tasty home-grown tomatoes? It's been done. How about horticulture therapy for trauma victims? Hydroponic gardens in space vehicles? Composting in a bucket for the city gardener? These are marketable twists.

Put A New Twist on a Tired Topic

What if you've got a topic that's relevant, but you've seen it covered before? Then put a new twist on it by interviewing experts, finding people who have experienced the topic, experiencing it yourself, or (if appropriate) adding a recipe. (See Food and Cooking in Chapter 7). You may have a great idea for an article on backyard gardening and using fresh vegetables. Ho-hum. Now give it a fresh snap and share your grandmother's recipe for Juarez-style salsa.

Another way to twist a piece into a new article is to slant the material to a new audience. To do this, you'll need to keep your reader clearly in mind. Go back and study past issues of the publications you're going to query, review the magazine's advertisements, be sensitive to the reader of that publication and you'll increase the chances of a sale. For instance, including grandmother's Juarez-style salsa recipe, above, might discount you with a publication that never uses recipes—or only Asian recipes. Be smart and double check that you're using the right slant with the right magazine.

If you're selling second serial or reprint rights for an article that's been published, you need to tell the magazine's editor that your article has been in print. If, however, you're significantly changing the article, using new quotes from experts, adding how-to sidebar material, etc., you have essentially created a new article. Then you need not tell the editor, "Once a few years ago, I wrote an article on a similar topic."

Freshen Previously Published Material

If rewriting articles and producing spin-offs are twenty-four carat gold, reselling articles is platinum. You make more money for doing nothing more than sending the article out to another magazine. Passive income? Almost. It takes time to organize, but once the system is established, it brings in bucks. I like to think of reselling articles as icing on a cake. You can live without it, but it's still very good.

A sizeable number of magazines are buying reprints, articles that have been printed in non-competing publications because the magazines can pay less and editing is already complete. To find magazines that buy reprints, check with writer's marketing books and verify the fact with the magazine's writer's guidelines or by a call to the editor.

When reselling articles, be up front about the fact that the article has been previously sold and copyrights have been reverted back to you for the sale of second rights. Be prepared to furnish information on the first magazine, editor's name and the date when it was originally published.

To sell a previously published article, first locate a magazine that buys reprints, make a sharp photocopy of the article, and send the article along with a short cover letter and a SASE. Print or type your name, address, phone, e-mail address and social security number on top of the article. Depending on the magazine and your relationship with its editor, send a letter listing other reprints you have available. Again include that SASE if you want a response.

Foreign publications are excellent markets for reprints. Check with the international version of *Literary Market Place* for specific magazines, visit an international book and magazine store (international airports and metropolitan newsstands are a good source for these magazines) and subscribe to a writer's newsletter that covers international publications.

Another good market for reprinted articles in your own community are the local publications, such as the one published by your chamber of commerce or parks department. You may be paid  a lot less than other magazines, but once you've rewritten the article and published various spin-offs, a point is reached when you say, "enough!" Sell the article locally and you'll receive a bonus—a few more dollars for your checking account.

6

Six

RESEARCH METHODS — FIND IT FAST

*D*id you know there's a person in some obscure city in the United States who waits for you, the experienced writer, to make a microscopic mistake on your research, add a tiny fact that's not true, misquote an expert, use a slightly-stretched statistic? That "Fact Fanatic" calls or writes your editor to complain about sloppy journalism and your work instantly loses credibility. Worse, you may not get another assignment. The only solution is to become the consummate researcher.

Seriously complete and correct research adds validity to your work and sets you apart from other writers who don't care or don't know how to research. It's not hard to do a thorough job.

Research Without Pain and Anguish

Whether you're writing an article, newspaper column,

newsletter piece or advertorial, these steps will help you focus your research.

Step 1: Select a topic. Find a subject area you really care about. If you genuinely like the subject you're researching, the project will become a challenge rather than an ordeal.

Step 2: Narrow the subject to a manageable size. Keep the restrictions of your work in mind. For instance, if you're writing a lengthy article (say 5,000 words or more), you have more flexibility than if you're writing a short piece of 300 words.

Step 3: Write out your objective. What do you want to say to the reader? What points are you attempting to make? Ask yourself questions. You do not need to have the answers, yet.

Step 4: Select a working title. A working title helps keep research focused.

Step 5: Prepare and continue to update your bibliography. Keeping track of sources during the research is much easier than retracing your search at the end. Some magazine editors want your bibliography and/or your sources submitted with your article.

Step 6: Prepare a working outline. Break your project down into major areas, using various outline techniques, including the "Bubble Method" found in Chapter 5. It's okay if you still do not have enough research; mark your outline as to where you need to fill in the blanks.

Step 7: Take notes. Use note cards or a search log journal to record quotes and valuable information. Keep information in a computer file or whatever works for you.

Step 8: Write the rough draft. Included will be:

> *Introduction:* Present the main idea, or thesis statement, in a way that the reader will want to continue reading, i.e., format the "hook."

> Write *the body:* Develop your main ideas and support them with details, quotes, anecdotes, and facts.

Write *the conclusion:* Summarize your ideas, restate your thesis.

Revise your draft: Check content, organization, spelling, experts' names, punctuation, etc.

Step 9: Write the final draft. If you're using a lot of foreign words, medical terms, names, statistics, etc., double check for correctness.

Forms of Research to Consider

Don't just stop with *Books in Print* or a web search when you're researching, look at the following:

Serials

Government documents

Pamphlets

Theses and dissertations

Patents

Translations

Annual reports

Bibliographies

Guides to the literature and directories

Other research sources include: Autobiographies, eye-witness reports (such as those found in old newspapers), diaries, church and family records, historical accounts in specialty museums, census reports, questionnaires, and experiments.

Don't overlook the most obvious form of research: Your own experience. For an article about the work they do, imagine interviewing Border Patrol agents. Sounds okay, right? Now think of how it would feel to spend a day as a "ride-along" in a Border Patrol jeep or car, really talking to the agents who must put their lives on the line. Now that's research that's marketable.

Getting Help with Research

Need help? Then clear communication is the key because if you can't quite fathom what information you're seeking, it's going to be tough to talk about it. Learning how to communicate to attain research is simple. Ask questions.

There are lots of ways to format research questions. Some will help you get information; others will stymie the process. To aid the flow of communication between you and the information specialist (the librarian, research assistant, curator), format questions in the following manner. The words and phrases underlined indicate the specifics of the information that is being sought:

1. <u>Limit and description</u>: "I need information on the <u>eating habits</u> of <u>15 year-old girls</u> who attended <u>public school</u> in <u>New York State</u> during the <u>last five years</u>. I would like <u>journal</u> <u>articles</u>, <u>documents</u>, <u>research reports</u> and/or <u>books</u> on the subject. I am <u>writing a magazine article</u> for an <u>educational magazine</u>.

2. <u>Duplication of effort</u>: "I would like materials on innovative landscaping programs that use recycled materials. I have checked the *Reader's Guide to Periodic Literature*, *Los Angeles Times Index* and *The New York Times Index*, all of which have been helpful. Will you help me find additional information <u>that was published in the last three years</u>?

3. <u>Perception of the investigation area:</u> "Would you help me find the enrollment figure for exceptional children in elementary schools in Ohio for the year 1997? <u>By exceptional, I mean, those who have some physical impediment which causes them to be treated differently from other children</u>.

4. <u>Time designation</u>: "I would like a copy of Julia Cameron's book, *The Artist's Way*, published in 1992. I would like to have the book <u>within a week</u>.

5. <u>Adequate information for prompt search</u>: "In the *Christian Science Monitor*, November, 1997, <u>Dr. Chris Smith</u> wrote an article presenting views on <u>animal-assisted emotional</u>

<u>therapy in the United States</u>. How can I find/arrange to obtain a photocopy of the article?

When asking for information, communicate what you need and want, and you'll get it. Don't be put off if the librarian says, "Sorry, I can't help you." Ask: Who can help? Where *can* I find more information?

Evaluating Research on the Internet

The Internet is nearly an essential tool for all writers. On the Internet, anyone can be a publisher, an expert, an authority. Some people create authentically appearing material just for fun, or to snag your interest. As a writer, you'll have to differentiate the quality, suitability, originality of sources and authenticity of that material.

Here are some tips on the evaluation process:

Depth and Scope: When evaluating the depth and scope of an Internet source, see how complete the coverage is. Has the author listed all sources or only his or her favorite sources? Are the major areas covered or only a smattering?

Source: Where did the material originate? Are there any facts, statistics, quotes attributed to another source that are verifiable? If sources are not verifiable, is the source worth using? Be suspicious; numbers and facts can be manipulated.

(Internet sources provided by the government, well-known non-profit agencies, and major corporations are typically of higher quality.)

Degree of Quality Control: The quality material is tough to assess unless you know something about the topic. If you're not that far yet, look for clues such as typos, grammatical errors, or suspicious connections with other sources. If the experts who are from major companies or on staff at universities have put their name on material, it assures that the researcher has some degree of quality.

Currency: It would seem, initially, that anything on the

Internet should be up-to-the-minute. Not so. Sometimes material stays on the Internet because it's been forgotten. Unlike books with the copyright date printed in the front, it's not always easy to tell when a citation or source was created or updated. You may have to cross-reference to other material that is current to find out the currency of the research you've discovered on the Internet.

Research Strategy

•Decide *generally* what your topic will be; don't hesitate to jot down other possibilities. Sometimes the best ideas branch off when you least expect them.

•Survey the literature of your field. Make sure you understand unfamiliar terms.

•Decide what kind of sources you'll use: Primary, or secondary. Try to calculate how much material you will need. Typically, you'll need more than you think you will.

•Decide what level of authority you'll need to consult. Scholarly? Popular? What other sources can you use?

•Budget your time. Ask for assistance from others who may have information. If you still hit a brick wall, ask: "Where might I find more information?"

•Become Mr./Ms. Sherlock Holmes. The facts are out there; you just have to find the clues to put the whole story together.

If you can't find enough information you have choices: 1) Go back to the beginning and start with another topic, or 2) Search deeper because you've discovered an area that hasn't been exploited by another writer.

Don't Overlook the Basic

Beginning writers shudder at the thought: "Why I'd never use an encyclopedia for research." Maybe that's why they have trouble researching. They forget that basic tools  help with basic tasks. Encyclopedias are perfect places to begin finding out about broad topics.

In the listings, you'll get an overview, statistics (as current as the edition you're using), and most likely where to find other information. No, you won't find up-to-the-minute data and that can be a drawback. But if you need to know when Empress Josephine established the first rose garden, when Arizona was admitted to the Union, or a short bio of Pancho Villa, an encyclopedia can come to a quick rescue.

Simple Steps to Avoid Plagiarism

Step 1: Begin researching immediately. Waiting until near the due date of your article can muddle the decision-making process, with: "Gee, could I really get away with using this exactly as it's printed?"

Step 2: Be selective. When writing an article, tackle a topic you're interested in. If you find the research boring, there's a tendency to do a second-rate job or snatch information from others' works.

Step 3: Understand what you're reading. Ask a librarian or other expert to decipher the information if it's too complex.

Step 4: Turn your ideas into words, your own words. Combine the words with your thoughts and experiences.

Step 5: Take notes paraphrasing and summarizing. Create fresh ways of providing the research.

Step 6: Don't be afraid to use direct quotes. Make sure you're quoting the original source accurately, with appropriate citations.

Step 7: Formalize your topic sentence; make sure that your conclusion fulfills the topic sentence's promise.

Search Logs

Call it kismet, Universal Guidance, or Whatever, once you begin to research your topic, material will flow to you. To keep track of this windfall, you'll want to organize it in a search log.

A search log is a list of research. Included are the materials you've accessed, the result of your search, and notes you've accumulated during the search. It is a daily/weekly journal of what you've accomplished in the research process.

There are plenty of ways to organize a search log—a paper trail—that will allow you to document sources and relocate and cite supporting details for your book or magazine article.

Some writers keep a three-ring binder of material, others jot the information in journals, and some prefer to keep it on a computer file. A fourth group throws it all in a pile until it's time to write (dangerous but it does work).

In the front of your log, keep a working outline of your project. It's helpful to date the material. With each entry:

1. Write the elements of the citation. *For books*: Author, title, place of publication, publisher and date. *For periodicals*: Author, title of article, title of periodical, issue number, volume number, date. *For electronic media*: Author (or group), date of publication, title, location including access information.

2. Note where the source came from (which library, person, television program, etc.).

3. List other sources that were of no value. Should you have to revisit a research source for more information, going back to useless ones is a major time waster.

4. Take notes with each entry (or photocopy material and provide a code in the search log correlating to the copied material.

5. On the notes, include paraphrases of information,

direct quotes, and summaries. Keep the notes linked with other information.

6. List the names of people contacted/interviewed (including how to reach them again and double check all spelling).

7. Add your thoughts, observations and conclusions.

More Tips on Research

Just because you think it's commonplace to know the makings for matzos, your reader might not. When doing research, be sure to define terms and buzz words that might be unfamiliar to you or your reader. You'll need to clarify ideas in a way that your reader will understand, keep bibliographic citations in case you need to go back to the material or verify the information, and list the names of people contacted/interviewed. You never know when you'll have to or want to return to the information to reuse it for spin-offs.

Depending on your topic, don't overlook the special collections some libraries have. For example, court records of 1850-1865, from Cleveland, Ohio, might give a clue to those involved in the Underground Railroad. Early city maps from Los Angeles might show where the original Spanish ranchos were located. To use historical societies, private libraries, or academic collections, special approval is sometimes required. Sometimes there's a fee.

Citing Internet and Other Sources

Citations are a method of acknowledging credit and academic debt. Citations provide a way for readers to trace the source of your material. Citations give readers a way to get more information on your topic. For technical and academic articles, you may be required to submit a bibliography that will be printed in the magazine. For non-technical articles, the magazine editor may still want you to submit a bibliography of your research sources. *Chicago Manual of Style* provides all the details on how to cite printed sources; libraries and bookstores have it.

Unlike published sources found in print, there is no current "perfect" way to cite an Internet source. If the magazine's editor wants a specific format, that's the one to use. Generally, you'll want to include:

• Author of a particular work (this may be the department, university or organization)

• Date of publication (If there is only an e-mail message or Usenet newsgroup posting, use this date.)

• Title of the resource (The title may be the posting message.)

• The location of the research on the Internet (Include the type of Internet resource, i.e., e-mail, URL, etc.)

Here are examples of citation of Internet information:

Winter, Mark. (1997). *WebElements* [World Wide Web]. Available: http://www.shef.ac.uk/uni/academic/A-C/chem/web-elements/web-elements-home.html

National Association of Press Photographers. (1998, January 12) *National Press Photographers Association* [World Wide Web]. Available: http://sunsite.unc.edu/nppa

Here's an example of an electronic source citation:

Wood, Daniel B., "Largest Welfare-to-Work Program Called a Success," *USA Today*, December 27, 1997. Located in CD NewsBank (Compact Disc,) NewsBank Inc.

Seven

MARKETING YOURSELF AND SELLING YOUR WRITING

*H*ere's what you've been waiting for—a "What's Hot" list of the popular magazine article types. What type of articles really sell? Can you focus on one magazine writing genre and be nearly guaranteed to sell your work (as long as you produce salable copy)? Yes. You can.

The What and Why of Salable Articles

Generally, how-to articles are the easiest to sell to magazines. Readers (and editors know this) have an affair with how-tos. Magazine editors know this and work to satisfy this need. How-tos have been hot for years, and they'll remain so well into the new century. You can bank on that.

Don't ignore the possibilities of writing how-tos, even if at first glance, you might consider a magazine far too sophisticated to buy a fundamental piece.

Years ago I wrote and sold an article to *Surfer Magazine*. The topic wasn't a specific surfing technique—I don't surf. Rather, it focused on how to buy a surfboard. While the magazine looks like it's geared to the accomplished surfer, smart editors know advertisers depend upon attracting new participants to the sport. Some of those new readers are also new to the sport and may not know how to buy a board. The magazine editor jumped at my query, and they were pleased with the manuscript. They never even asked if I could swim or surf because I could obviously write from a consumer's viewpoint.

Expand your knowledge base

This point was brought home recently when my son left a copy of *Mountain Bike* magazine on the coffee table. Like most writers, I'll read anything. As I flipped through the pages, one article hit me. It was titled something like: "Good Food for Bikers." It was a basic, uncomplicated article on sound nutrition. Sure there were buzz words for those who ride mountain bikes, but if you changed the words, it could have been slanted for any sport. Popular magazines need specific articles for the seasoned enthusiast and simple articles for the beginner. Don't overlook the obvious.

Although you may already have begun specializing in one type of magazine article, be sure to read the rest of this chapter. Open your mind to new genres, especially if you're determined to increase your checking account and see your name in print more often. I've outlined the "best bet" article types in detail and real ways to make them work and that will make your job easier.

The How-To and Self-Help Articles

The how-to article is the most used format in today's magazines. Self-help articles use the same simple formula. As the name implies, a self-help is oriented to personal needs while a how-to teaches or provides information. They do cross over.

Topics for this genre range from how to adopt a baby and how to split a cord of wood to technical articles for software encryptors to step-by-step directions for developing on-line 3-D monsters intended to be read by computer animators. It's good to spend time flipping through *Reader's Digest* and noting how most of the articles begin in the ways indicated below. This magazine and almost all others that use this basic formula do so because it works.

Here's what you need to know:

Start with the beginning: Most articles start with using a strong "hook" (the words that immediately get the reader involved) and then yank that hook and make the reader care.

Therefore, the first paragraph should include one of the following "hooks":

- A quote from a notable person, an expert. (An expert is a person who has experience on the topic. A fire fighter is an expert on forest fires and arson; a dentist is an expert on tooth and gum health, a child is an expert on toys, games and playground manners.)

- A statistic that captures the reader's interest, i.e.: Seven out of eight writers believe they are physically and mentally addicted to the craft of writing.

- A strong thesis statement, such as: When a best friend moves away, your child may have her first experience with grief.

- You can ask a question—ask a number of questions. This is a sure-fire way to start an article, i.e.,: Is your spouse faithful? Or: What is your cat telling you? Or: Could a letter bomb be delivered to *your* mailbox?

Move to the middle: Here you'll want to focus on three to ten main topics, depending on the depth and length of your article.

- Give an overview of what you'll cover. Number

your points, if only for your information, and then change the numbers to bullets or subtopics later.

- Use clear, tight sentences. Sentences over three lines are probably too long for contemporary magazines. Likewise, paragraphs over fifteen lines of text written for popular publications need to be broken up.

- State your premise and give examples to validate your points either from personal experience or through experts' quotes.

Now end the how-to or self-help article. To do so, resolve the points.

- You'll want to give hope, provide a solution, focus on how much better life will be when the situation is resolved. You can also end with a quote from your expert or finish the anecdote introduced in the beginning of the article.

- (If the ending is awkward, review your topic sentence idea. Restate the premise. Rewrite it. Put in some punch and you'll have the summary.)

Even short pieces have this potential

Think sidebar material—tantalizing thoughts or ideas you didn't have room for in the article are perfect for the sidebar. Sometimes I save an important topic, directions, or a bit of supplemental information for the sidebar. Depending on your topic, you may want to include inspirational concepts, motivational tips, examples with anecdotes, interviews, statistics, and/or recommendations.

How-to articles range in length depending on the publication and your assignment. An article "How to Choose a Rose" could be written in 50 to 100 words and would work well for a how-to newsletter that would be sold at gardening shops. Now look at the rose piece again. This time imagine you queried and were assigned this same piece for a horticulture magazine such as *American Rose Magazine*. Fifty words would probably be useless to rose-knowledgeable readers. For *American Rose,* you'd want to have an overview of varieties, how to select the best for your region, and maybe a rundown on those that require less water or winterization. As a sidebar, you could list the names and toll free numbers of rose catalogues or the intriguing history of buying roses from catalogues.

That's how easy it is to turn a modest how-to topic of 50 words into 2000 words, and with the freelancer's fee increased accordingly.

Self-help articles tell the reader how to help themselves. Topics are as varied as "The First Steps to Save Your Life" (an article about walking after a heart attack) to "Is There Love After the Honeymoon?" (steps to continue the romance of marriage well beyond the first year).

To sell how-to and self-help articles, focus on:

• writing the topic and text. Slant it to the readership of the magazine.

• using a slant that's either unique or one that's basic.

Interviews and Personality Profiles

Have you had the opportunity to interview someone for something you're writing about? Was it successful or mediocre or scary? Chapter 5 provides almost-never-fail interviewing tips. If you're doing an interview tomorrow, review that section now.

Interview and personality profile articles are popular, making them rank third in salability. Knowing how, when, and why to interview can establish you as a hot magazine writer.

People are interviewed because they are experts or they have something to say. The expert or "subject" is the person to be interviewed, also some writers call the topic of an article the "subject." The subject of an article for *Money* may have parlayed a small inheritance into enough for retirement. The person you might interview for *Motor Trend* may have designed a new electric system that never fails. Your "expert" may have been there for a natural disaster or an award, been part of history or a riot, worked for a cause or was a cause for national concern. Do you see how easy it can be? Experts are everywhere.

Always take time to study any magazine for which you plan to write. Nine out of 10 times you'll see interviews. Some articles contain more than one expert interviewed in each article.

Profiles, also called "Personality Pieces," are little more than mini-biographies, normally highlighting one facet of the individual's life. An article in *Daughters of Sarah* might highlight the life and work of a local soup kitchen or a urban day care center. A piece in *Crochet Digest* could talk with a winner of a county fair crocheting contest, and include the how and why he took up the hobby after retirement.

You're most likely familiar with personality pieces that provide tantalizing bits about our favorite movie stars, authors, sports figures, and politicians. These pieces give an insider's look at experts in specific occupations with unique lifestyles.

Some years ago, I had the opportunity to interview Vidal Sassoon. As you may remember, it was Sassoon who changed the role of hairdressers and hairstyles around the world. No one before or after  Sassoon can make this claim to fame. And there I was—the first journalist he'd granted an interview with in seven silent years. The article I produced was a personality piece combined with an interview feeling, an intimate view of the great hair designer. All my questions were focused on a personal view of his work in London and those of his time. (He was a contemporary of the Beatles and dress designer Mary Quant. He routinely mingled with the super cool stars of the rock and roll '60s.)

I organized my questions to reflect what my readers would want to know if *they* had been sitting with Sassoon. I compared the past to his work with humanitarian causes. The article turned out well because I fulfilled my own curiosity and turned it into words the reader wanted to read.

You have lots of creative freedom when writing the interview or personality profile. Your chief focus? Bring out information that the consumer wants. Be their eyes and ears. Write about the person, the subject, in a special way. Find a twist and make the copy come alive. Whether you make it silly or serious or dotted with fizzing fluff, all will depend on the publication and readership at which you've aimed your article's ambition.

The only dictate for this genre is to make your piece correct. Everything else is up to you and the editor from what you think of as good taste to use of sensationalism.

The Question and Answer Article

The question and answer article, also know as Q&A, is always popular and regularly used for expert and celebrity articles.

To "pull it off well," write down all your questions. Use yes and no questions and open-ended questions, too. For instance, you could ask: Did you enjoy living near the Arctic Circle? Or you could ask: What was it like not to see the sun for months on end? How did it affect you emotionally? What about your kids? Your pets?

Make some questions more difficult to answer. Be sure to ask if there are other topics your subject would like to include.

If appropriate, give your subject the questions before the interview. When I was recently the subject of an article in the *Catholic Twin Circle*, I asked for the list of questions beforehand so that I could provide statistics and in-depth answers. I didn't want to come off as glib or unprepared. Don't think you're being accused of being a beginner if you're asked to supply questions; my reporter had received numerous awards for his writing, yet I still wanted those questions for me.

Have a theme or focus for the article, and design your questions to support the theme. If your subject isn't well known, include a short bio or have the subject talk about her/his experience in that field.

Don't just write out the responses. That's where novice writers go wrong—and they don't make a sale. Once you've transcribed the interview, your work begins. Make the "conversation" absorbing, engrossing reading. Make it worthy of your reader's time.

Informational and Consumer Awareness Articles

These articles types are on America's most wanted article lists. They are the providers of information and consumer awareness. Sometimes referred to as service articles, I've separated them because they provide information, yet typically they don't tell how to do anything in the strictest sense.

Examples of informational articles are "Sex By Phone: What Numbers are Your Kids Calling," to the *Reader's Digest* articles that might include "Designer Estrogens," "Updates in Plastic Surgery," and "Mutual Fund Scams."

Ever flip through a magazine and read an article that seemed more like an advertisement that an informational piece? You've just read an advertorial—that is an article that really plugs a product or service. They are common in all popular magazines. They are advertising that's written in a way that it looks much more like editorial copy.

Consumer awareness articles are just that: They make the public aware. They focus on issues from spray-can pollutants to deadly baby carseats. Topics for consumer awareness articles that might be sold to *Your Health & Fitness* could be: "What Blood Test Numbers Really Mean," "Toenail Fungus— Help is Here," or "Are You Ready for a Laser Face Lift?"

The trick here is to hook the reader at once. You have just seconds before the reader turns the page. There are no statistics on this, but you may have even less time when you write to an editor to query about submitting an article. We're talking about 30 seconds. To write these pieces you must verify all facts and come to a strong conclusion in this category. If you fail to follow through, the editor won't buy.

As you review magazines that use this genre, take mental note of the sidebars (separate mini-articles), supporting one topic in your main article. They're often used in this category. Not too long ago I wrote an article for *San Diego Parent* on fun and inexpensive things to do with kids. It was for a summer issue that was slanted toward parents who had more time than money. I included a sidebar that had a list of San Diego museums where kids could get in free. I could have included this information in the article itself, but it made a nifty sidebar which supported my article well.

For consumer awareness articles, you'll want to present additional sources of information; for example the names, telephone number and addresses, support groups or lobbies, or various free pamphlets offered through these and manufacturing companies on the topic. This can be done with a sidebar or as part of your article.

Inspirational and Religious Articles

Do you have what it takes to inspire or write about your personal beliefs? Then you and this category should match well.

These articles run from highly orthodox pieces for *The Christian Century* to less traditional ones found in *Moment: Jewish Educational Venture* and *Guidepost*. Further, inspirational articles can be found in *Redbook, Modern Romances*, and *Catalist*. You might find one in the magazine produced by your alumni association or the credit union affiliated with your employer.

Before writing inspirational and religious articles, it's wise to review the publication. For instance with *Moment* mentioned above, one might think they take stuffy stuff, when in fact, lively writing is a prerequisite for a sale to this magazine. Also know the terms of the genre and how they are used. Do the periodical's readers prefer being known as fundamentalist or spirit-filled beings? You'll need to use the terms correctly to make a sale.

Most inspirational and religious magazines are *extremely nice* to writers so don't hesitate to query if you have a perfect idea. Their editors go out of their way to help and share information. If you enjoy this genre, can use the lingo, and write in the style that's preferred, you can achieve a fine, regularly selling position.

Humor Articles

While humor is subjective, most magazines will use a piece that's well written and slanted to their readership. As other writing teachers do, I always stress that writing humor is a skill that can be learned, but it takes an expert writer to do it well. Humor isn't everyone's cup of java.

I'm always surprised when someone tells me how funny an article I've written was, or how amusing some words I've put together are. Why? I love to read it, but find writing humorous pieces a tough way to make a living. Luckily, some of us have the knack. I've talked with people who write humor and they say, "I never force it—it's just bubbles up." Or, "Humor happens."

As exacting as it is to be able to write words that make people chuckle, you may want to give it a try. Why? Because humor is hot and it sells. Stop for a moment or two and look around your house or office. Look at magazines from *Outdoor Action* to *Dis"ability" Magazine*. These and thousands of others buy humor and fill their pages with good laughs.

Do you have that gift to take everyday situations and turn them into written gags? Then hop to. Remember, also, not all humor is of the side-splitting variety. There's humor that makes you feel warm inside and there's humor that makes you cringe. The only rule is that you elicit a quirky emotion in the reader.

Humor is subjective and today there are as many types of humor as there are styles of clothing. When writing a query letter, for instance, you can't just say: I want to submit a funny article on my trip to Baltimore. You'll have to write a bit of humor about Baltimore within that letter of inquiry. Give the flavor of the piece to instantly tickle the editor's funny bone.

As-Told-To Articles

Either you love these articles or you pass them by. America, in general, thinks they're great so if you can write as-told-to articles you can mine for gold right here. These pieces are the basis for women's magazines, the tabloids, and confession magazines.

As the name indicates, as-told-to articles give the name of the individual who had the experience with the writer's name following it, sometimes in smaller print. Most of the as-told-to articles feature some trauma and how the individual survived.

What can you do to increase the odds of selling as-told-to articles? Do your research well. Start with an interview with the person who is to tell the story. Query editors with facts and irresistible quotes. Make the article lively and entertaining. Make sure you've got all the facts straight.

Travel Articles

Travel articles have become increasingly difficult to sell, but magazines still buy them by the score. The difference?

Writers today can't simply take a nice trip, write about it, and sell it. Today, you have to really know a place, and make it irresistible, then "frost it" with a universal message. Read travel articles and analyze how they're formatted. Here are some tips.

1. Write about places you know and love or would like to visit. Research the places well.

2. Choose one location/area and become an expert on it.

3. Look at well-traveled places with a new twist/slant. Dig out a little known detail (historical, cultural, contemporary) and work it into the piece.

4. Describe the place with enough of the big picture that the reader knows where he/she is, but with tidbits that make it fascinating for someone who has been there before.

5. When visiting a location or even your hometown, ask questions. Get involved with the people, do local stuff, visit a family, go to the market or bazaar, sit on the dock, attend a festival. Smile and become a tourist.

6. Double check facts, including the spelling of location names and historical figures. Define foreign or unfamiliar words or terms.

7. Take photos. Offering photos can increase the possibility of sale and produce extra money, too. (Take a quick class in photography or watch one of the photography videos until you know what you're doing.)

8. If some part of your trip has been difficult or especially memorable, tell your reader. Think sidebar material, too.

9. Choose your title with care. Make it appealing but tell the reader where he/she is about to go.

10. Realize that some travel pieces are also how-tos, food and cooking articles, and personal essays.

Food and Cooking Articles

Americans are obsessed with food (and spirits); the lore, the taste, the ambience. It's more than just good eats and drinks; food and cooking articles feed magazines. Editors are hungry for this category. You don't have to be a great cook to write about food, but you must be a good writer and write as though you like food and/or drink.

What's the key to success in food and cooking articles? It sounds gooey, but you must produce "drool copy." If you write in this genre, you'll have to get the editor salivating with a smashing title and a delicious query. Do so, and you've made a sale.

• The food and cooking article is normally a how-to piece, yet it can be an essay or Q&A. I've also seen food and cooking articles in religious publications and entertainment magazines. It has a lead, a middle, and a punchy conclusion.

The article might concern beverages, appetizers, main dishes, and so on, or the places, people, countries, or history of the food. It might also give the background or helpful growing hints on producing the ingredients, such as growing herbs on your kitchen windowsill. Additionally, this article type often surrounds the concept of food with other ideas. It might focus on one food (lemons, chocolate, ice cream, pasta), season, or facet of food or spirits.

• Research the magazine before you write the query. For instance, one magazine might take recipes along with historical tidbits of food preparation. Another may want straight recipes and no text, no extra information about who is eating or interested in this food.

• Tie this article type in with the seasons/events. How about "Hearty Winter Soups that Fill You Up, But Not Out," "Old-Fashioned Bride's Cakes," or "Fabulous Fat-Free Valentine's Cookies." Special events from baby showers and bar mitzvahs, tailgate parties to cocktail parties all warrant food articles.

• Spot trends in eating and move quickly. Articles on low-fat cooking were unheard of ten years ago; now they're the stock and trade of most every women's magazine you see at the store. Family recipes/nostalgia are always popular and don't go out of fashion—especially with a new twist. You might have article material right in your recipe box if you can produce an article about Grandmother's Cinnamon Tarts, or something along this line.

• When submitting recipes, be brief but precise.

• Do you have a great article idea, but can't seem to sell it? Turn it into a food and cooking article, and it will probably sell like, well, hot cakes.

Personal Essays

Soap box. Potent cause. Humorous moment. Americana. Slice-of-life. These, and others, are the personal essays you read in popular magazines.

You needn't be a humor writer to sell personal essays. See the world in your own way and make it interesting or provocative for someone else and you have a personal essay.

Many major magazines, from *Vim & Vigor* to *Yankee* have places for essays. Here are some tips to make them work:

• Stay focused on your message

• Add thoughtful/colorful/funny examples

• Don't tell all the mundane details

• Make the message universal enough to reach a wide readership

• Arrive at some basic truth

• Get your reader involved; use emotions and word pictures

• Pick an experience you care about; you can't fake this

• Don't make publication your primary goal

- Steer clear of the essay to vent anger, indignation, or negative emotions
- Have the courage to reveal yourself honestly
- Show what you've gone through; don't tell it in steps
- Use personal essay to inform, educate and entertain

Bottom line? Look at the world honestly, with a fresh eye to humanity's quirks, and you've got a personal essay worth publication. If you want to aim for fame in this genre, read every essay you can and practice writing them before you submit.

Op-Ed: Those Opinion Articles

Some new writers might consider these "just letters to the editor." They are and more—they're good ways to add to writing credits. Op-Ed pages in the newspaper, and personal statements with topics like "Let's Take Back Our Neighborhoods from Gangs" make a writer's work visible.

If you want to produce a publishable Op-Ed piece, make your goal to convince the reader (and the editor initially) that what you have to say is important. Remember, winning arguments over a cup of coffee or a beer doesn't make one a good writer of Op-Ed.

To produce Op-Ed, you'll have to take a stance on a topic and then prove your point. You might want to read that opinionated guy, Dave Barry, and get a feel for his work. Remember, he earned a Pulitzer Prize for his opinion pieces.

Sure they're fun to read, and the opinion pieces reveal the conviction of the writers. In order to write for the Op-Ed page, the article must flow with strong paragraphs and words that are produced to involve the reader. You must make a reader care—and you can use humor to do it—Dave does.

Entertainment Articles

Do you want to write pieces that "entertain" others? You can do that with the basics discussed above, such as how-to articles, inspirational pieces, and personality profiles. You can go further and write articles to amuse, cheer, arouse, or divert the reader. As an example you might write an entertainment article about public art and performances in your community, a local weaver who gives lessons, or elephants or cats who paint.

These articles are often blends of reflection, opinion and perspective. If you enjoy entertainment and the arts, revel in your passions and stay on top of trends and the people who make the headlines (even in your own community).

Consider becoming a reviewer or critic and offer reviews to magazines. Look at the magazines you enjoy and come up with a letter asking about reviewing something you feel strongly about—a brash rock group that started in your neighborhood, a dinner theater that focuses on *comédie noir*, a book that sets your nerves tingling.

The next step is to contact the editor with your ideas on the book or performance. In your letter, be specific as to why you're qualified to write the review and pour on the persuasion.

Or write the review and send it to the editor. Keep in mind that I live by the law of queries. If an editor likes what I have to say in a query letter, he or she will want to see the review or article.

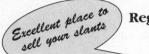
Excellent place to sell your slants

Regionals and Newspapers

Does your community have a newspaper? Are there "disposable" magazines stacked right inside the health-food store, the video store, or the library? Does the local Chamber of Commerce publish a magazine? These publication may now be "throwables" to the beginner, but are valuable to the savvy writer. And some pay quite well. If you're just beginning in writing, the periodicals above are an excellent place to publish and get clips (samples of printed articles).

Next time you're walking into a member discount store, pick up one of their magazines. Begin collecting regional publications and formatting ideas for their special readership. For instance in southern California, FedCo, a large membership store, uses short pieces (300 to 500 words) on events and historical happenings. Recent issues included a charming piece about the "First Orange Tree in Riverside County." Another regional magazine had a story about the bulb farms in Holland, Michigan.

Regardless of where you live, there's a regional magazine or newspaper that would like your work. You must, however, target your writing to their specific readership.

Fillers

Fillers can be great sources of income for savvy writers. These tiny bits of article material are typically anecdotes, light verse, narratives, household hints, tips for consumers and slice of life vignettes. Need an example? What about *Reader's Digest's* "Campus Comedy?" Like those who produce humor, writers who can do fillers have to be expert wordsmiths. No words can be wasted.

With fillers, you don't query a magazine. They're produced on speculation—you're counting on your ability to sell without promises beforehand. With fillers it's a fact of life.

Fillers sell for $5.00 to well over $500 depending on the subject, personality interview, or current event and the magazine in which they appear. Fillers are also an excellent way for a less-published writer to become established as a dependable magazine contributor. A byline of *Good Housekeeping* for a short poem or a quip will bolster any writer's credibility and ego, too.

Electronic Articles

If you're currently hooked on electronic magazines, you'll want to write for them. Many writers specialize in this field. To do so, contact the magazine via mail or e-mail and get the writer's guidelines. Read current issues, focus queries (which will be transmitted via your modem) and get to it.

If you haven't reviewed the magazines available on the Web, a good jumping off point is found by browsing through the home pages of various publications, data information services, or news libraries. For instance, a service called News library contains the full text of over 2,300 newspapers, newswires, newsletters and broadcast transcripts. Publications provided by News library include everything from *The New York Times* to *Le Monde* to *Africa News*.

Marketing and Placing Articles

Let's take a "tour" of a magazine office. Depending on your relationship with a magazine's editorial staff and where you live, you'll profit by taking a "field trip" to an magazine's office. You may be in for a shock—I was the first time I visited an editor at *Let's Live* in Los Angeles. It only took two minutes for me to realize why things get lost and queries take months to be answered. The old offices were piled nearly ceiling high with paper, magazines, books, photographs. Apparently their "filing" system worked because the magazine turns out well each month, but on first glance, the place was chaotic.

As I learned after working with many magazines, most are housed in small, cramped offices. Every flat surface is covered with stacks of materials piled according to some obscure system. Everyone on staff has three different jobs. The editor may not even have a private office. The editor's desk may be littered with this month's copy or budget projections which have to be completed by ten o'clock tomorrow morning. The editor probably has little time for lunch, has a love/hate relationship with the stacks of queries that arrive daily, and sometimes forgets to appreciate advertisers who continue to clamor for a price break on page layouts.

This same overly-stressed individual would feel absolutely blessed to be able to include a talented, dependable writer like you on the magazine's regular string of writers. Keep that last sentence in mind as you design your queries and call a busy editor for a status report.

So how does this process work? Let's look at it from query to the finished, published article. Once you have received a response to your query, you'll be sent a contract or a letter of acknowledgement outlining what copyrights are being purchased, the length of the article, the date that the article is due and whether you're to supply photographs or illustrations. Or you may have to confirm the assignment, as recommended previously.

Should you hit a snag, such as one of the experts you planned to interview becomes unavailable and your deadline is out of the question, contact the editor immediately to explain the circumstances. Give the editor options so that (hopefully) you will not lose the assignment. Editors are a storehouse of information. Ask for advice. Don't make it a habit, but think of the editor as a resource.

Sometimes magazines require freelancers to supply the names, telephone numbers and addresses of the experts they quote and/or the original source for facts. Don't be offended; this is simply a policy to protect the integrity of the publisher. For your own sake, keep a copy of the research list because as you rewrite the article for another market, you may need that information again.

More and more magazines are asking for articles to be sent via e-mail. Before you do it this way, make sure the magazine wants it electronically and exactly how they'll want the format produced. Some magazines may want you to send two hard (paper) copies of the manuscript and a disk; others want it faxed. Check with someone at the magazine's office or review the writer's guidelines for specific requirements.

In the transmittal of your manuscript, it's wise to include a *brief* cover letter and your invoice. If the article is written on spec, a self-addressed stamped envelope, with sufficient postage, should be included if the manuscript needs to be returned.

Some writers send manuscripts by certified mail. Some writers call the editor about a week after mailing a manuscript to be certain it has arrived. Some writers prefer to include a self-addressed postcard for the editor to note the date when the manuscript was received.

It's wise to keep a record of your submittals and the follow-up letters. If you write scores of queries and many articles each month, you'll require some type of recordkeeping system. Computers work well to keep track of the status of an article query. Talk to computer-literate writers about the software they use; check out their system and see if you can navigate it. While software works well, a pen and lined piece of paper are adequate at least to start.

You may want to keep a separate file on each query and article like the example below, or keep the status of all your manuscripts on one spreadsheet.

You'll probably want to list the topic/working title of the article or query, the date submitted and the result of your query. You might want to leave some space for a note, such as "Submit again in six weeks," or "Call editor after the first of the month for possible assignment."

Here's an example of a query record sheet:

Article Title	Date Submitted	Result
Stuff for Summer Fun		
Magazine A	3/9	Refused 3/21
Magazine D	3/9	Refused, but query again.
Magazine Z	3/9	Accepted, contract received 4/5, article due 4/29
Magazine X, 2nd rights	9/21	Sold 10/21

Keep a list of assignments, with all the pertinent information close to your typewriter or computer. It's an ego booster and helps organize your time. Estimate the amount of time it will take you to research, interview, and write each article. Rank them according to a priority system and organize your work load. It's great to have a lot of work, but terrible if you can't meet deadlines.

Marketing Ideas

Anytime you talk with seasoned writers, eventually the conversation will come around to identifying and using new and cross-markets to sell their work.

The big guys in magazines, *Time, Glamour, Woman's Day*, and *Sports Illustrated,* are excellent markets. Each day, they receive huge bundles of queries and unsolicited articles. As you target markets, it might be wise to assign a number to the desirability factor of each magazine and work down the list from the top to the lesser known ones. Or you may want to start marketing to the smaller publications immediately.

As an experienced writer, you may never sell or even want to sell to these major magazines. Why? Because the smaller magazines, the new periodicals, and the local publications are hungry for responsible, responsive, good writers. If you like

If you are fishing...go where they are biting

to be treated like a big fish, check out the smaller "ponds." With the smaller magazines, you may be able to establish a strong, core income. If you choose move to a bigger pond, you can use the smaller ones to acquire credibility.

Is there an old-fashioned magazine store in your area or a bookstore that seems to carry a wide selection of publications? Make friends with the owner, and ask to be told when a new magazine comes out. Perhaps your magazine seller will put a copy aside for you.

Read the publishing trade magazines for information on new publications. Browse through the magazines available at your library. Ask friends to save those advertisements for new magazines. The ads offer the subscription address; however with a little investigation, you'll be able to locate the editorial office address and phone number. Pour over the listings on magazines that appear in your writer's association newsletter.

The best writers seek out and analyze both new and old markets. A novice starts and ends with the magazines sold at the supermarket. An experienced writer knows the right twist on an article put to the right publication can be cross-queried and sold, and possibly sold again. For example, an article written for one of the New Age magazines on herbs used for healing might be salable to a magazine written for those interested in a health magazine, one for history buffs or a regional publication. Use the categories listed in writer's marketing books as a beginning for marketing your queries and articles.

And then recycle queries and write spin-offs. Those who are new to writing send out one query at a time. They wait for a positive reply. When it happens and an assignment comes their way, they creatively write the article, send it off, and eventually deposit the check. Fine and dandy. But this system could take years to make a year's worth of money.

The practiced writer turns that one article/idea into many by rewriting the basic article idea and writing spin-off pieces using one facet of the article on which to base a totally different article.

Since revising, spinning off, and rewriting articles means more money, success and credibility, why don't more writers do it? Simple. It's not easy. Beginners stop before they even consider the possibilities of rewriting for profit. Now that an article is written, it's time to put your rethinking cap back on and remarket your original idea with a new twist.

When you rewrite an article, you begin fresh, review your notes, look at your "bubbles" and check the web for updated information. Relisten to your tapes, and rejuvenate the material you've already polished. Sometimes, it's hard to dispose of your original golden words in order to revamp a piece. But that's exactly what you have to do if you want to recycle previously published material.

Why the work: It's easier to revise an article that has potential than to go through the entire research and writing process all over again on a totally different topic. Half the work is done when you rewrite an article or when you take the main topic and spin off in a different direction.

Scream out loud, but write spin-offs. This process is good for your career and your checking account. It's also good practice and the more you do it, the better you become.

From this minute forward promise me you'll look at every article with the possibility of turning it into eight, ten, or twenty different articles, fillers, columns and opinion pieces. An amusing anecdote from a scientist you talked with might reap $200 from a magazine that buys "quotable quotes" when submitted in a shorter version. It might be a perfect, humorous lead sentence for a scientific journal. A touching memory shared during an interview might be turned into an inspirational filler for *Catholic Life* or one of the romance magazines.

Should you have the time, the desire, and/or currently are without a score of contracted assignments for articles, go back over old articles whether they were sold or not. Reread them with an eye to what could be changed, updated or added. (Be sure to read about Food and Cooking Articles in this chapter.)

Jot down notes in the margins, and get ready to rewrite. Your goal is to turn material that's already been sold into a gold mine of your own making.

There is an art to marketing and you're going to like this "art" class if you like making money. Experienced writers know that writing without perceptive marketing isn't cost or energy effective, so they study the market and learn to sell their "product."

Every time you query a magazine, you are selling yourself, your background and training, and your potential as the best writer of an article. Here are some tips to consider to update your marketing strategies:

1. If your query or article on spec is rejected but you receive a gracious or (even somewhat) encouraging note from the editor, immediately review the magazine, study the market, and send another query to the editor or follow up with a brief phone call.

2. When submitting your manuscript as requested by an editor, send along at least one article idea or query. Always include a post card or SASE for a reply.

3. If you know the editor quite well and/or have written for the magazine before, you might want to bullet a number of topics, queries of about one paragraph in length, and submit the list. Your name, of course, belongs on that list. Include a SASE or stamped post card (with space for the articles they'd like to review) so that the editor can get back to you.

4. Should you call the editor or he or she calls you, have some topics available that you can talk about and talk up. This means you need to keep a file of enticing ideas near the phone, or desk, and be ready to slant the topic to the specific magazine. Sure it's nerve racking at first—that's why beginning writers don't do it.

5. Watch for editorial changes in the magazines you sub-

mit to so that you can contact the new editor or comment on the changes in format.

6. Read the letters to the editor portion of the magazines you query. You'll gain insight into what the magazine's readers want or don't want in articles.

7. Read books on marketing and sales. Digest books on increasing your creativity like Julia Cameron's *The Artist's Way*. And books on your profession like Bruce Keyes' *The Courage to Write*. Read books that inspire you to greatness whether the author is a Pulitzer prize winning writer or a Stanley Cup hockey player. Read books that allow you to know that old-fashioned respect and high ethical practices are as valid today as they were in the past. If you need a boost on simple yet enduring morality, read books from the *Chicken Soup* series.

Always remember, you're in sales. So what should you do if you get tongue-tied when you call an editor? Feel awkward when you talk about your work?

You need to practice a personal sales presentation so it works well over the phone, when you meet editors and interview experts. Try it in front of a mirror. Smile. Make your voice warm and your attitude approachable. How about videoing yourself in a "mock" interview (using a family member or even your child's stuffed toy as the expert). Definitely tape record to see how you sound on the telephone. If you think there's room for improvement, do so. A beginner would not make the effort because taking the "um" and "ah" filler words or slang expressions requires concentration, but in sales, little things give you the edge over the competition.

According to public speaking and sales experts, what you do and say within the first seven seconds of a conversation colors credibility. To gain confidence, join a public speaking group.  Toastmasters has an international reputation, and there are also speaking classes sponsored by community colleges and civic groups.

Every person you know is a potential expert, and every

editor has a network of others in the publishing business that just might need your services. It's up to you to ask for business if you want it. Yes, it sounds pushy, and at first it might feel uncomfortable, but since you don't advertise, you must let people know you are in the writing business. And you must network.

If you haven't done so yet, contact your local Chamber of Commerce and let them know you're a freelancer, and would like to be placed on their press release mailing list to receive new releases about celebrations and ceremonies scheduled for your town.

Publicity You Can Sell

Public relations firms are waiting and willing to assist the experienced writer to get their message out to the consuming public. They are especially helpful when you're planning to feature their client or product. Why do beginning writers refrain from contacting public relations firms? Because it takes nerve.

Public relations firms need writers, but novices don't realize that. They quiver with fear. As any experienced writer knows, you can write or call the PR firm with as many facts as possible to convince them that you will further their needs, getting the word out about their client, product or cause. And you won't charge them a cent. They'll love you.

Some years back, I was a contributing editor (a regular writer really, but that was my title) for *Fitness Today*. Although the publication isn't around anymore, at that time I wrote oodles of articles about how celebrities exercise and diet. My editor didn't care who the star of the month might be, just that he or she was fit, health conscious, and in the public eye. Being handsome or gorgeous helped too. I contacted some large PR firms in Los Angeles, sent copies of the magazine (the issues in which my byline appeared) and asked that someone contact me. I was deluged with mail and phone calls. I was popular and received 8x10 glossies of movie stars and sports figures. That simple contact method gave me enough famous people to write celebrity fitness articles for years.

It's not always that easy. It takes tenacity, and you must be prepared to sell yourself and the topic. But it can be done.

You also might find that you really enjoy rubbing elbows with the movers and shakers of the big and small screen. Celebrities are busy, but you'll quickly find out that movie and television people have plenty of time for journalists. That feels great. Besides the celebrity pieces are like blue chip stock—excellent material for fillers, quotes and spin-offs.

Don't be shy... celebs want exposure

Analyzing Tips to Increase Sales

As mentioned before, it's best to look at a publication you want to write for before you write a query to an editor. When you find the magazine, sit down and look it over using this plan.

1. Match the names on the masthead with the bylines on the articles.

2. Look at the list again. Do you see variations of names? M. Martin Smith could be Mary Smith, too. And Mary might be a staff writer. Although the publication might say it does accept freelance material, if you don't see non-staffers on the list, that might not be the case.

One of the magazines I worked for as a staff writer focused on the home improvement field. I wrote the entire magazine using various pen names. In theory it appeared that there were five different writers for each issue—untrue. Well you know.

If you can see that the magazine is only staff written, does this mean you shouldn't send a query? No. But you might want to call first. Magazine policies change, and your phone call could be timed just right to snag an assignment.

3.   Check the background of the authors of the articles. If the articles are written by people with advanced degrees and there aren't any by laypeople, most likely you'll be discounted unless you have the proper education.

4.   Compare the articles and the genres featured. What types of articles are found within those pages? How-tos on health? Interviews with leading religious leaders? Fun and frothy entertainment pieces? You'll just frustrate yourself if, for instance, you send a query on cooking with ginger to a magazine that only accepts article ideas on antique car parts. It's a silly comparison, but writers who don't take time to learn about a publication, in essence, do just that. They miss the mark completely.

5.   Who's used in the quotes? How many quotes are used? Can you get interviews from the same type of people for the article you'd write for the publication? If the answer is yes, you're right on target.

6.   Look at the length of the articles used. Some publications rarely use articles longer than 1,000 words—others top out at 500. If you send a query for an article on leaded glass craft projects and estimate it to be at 2,500 words and the publication only accepts 800 word pieces, you won't make a sale. This is true even if you've written a dynamite query.

7.   Look at the other features of the magazine. Do they have photos? What about sidebars? Do the articles have bullets or lists?

8.   Get clues from the advertisements. Looking at *Woman's Day* recently, there were advertisements for lawn care, coffee, cruises and collectible dolls. There were ads for high-fiber breads, salad dressing and carpet. On the inside of the back page was an ad for shampoo with the flip side of the sheet advertising a car.

As a writer who will make the grade, take this information and use it. With these topics alone, you could have a good idea of who buys the magazine. Look again at the paragraph above. This reader is a woman, a homeowner, and someone who has some discretionary income (enough to think of a cruise). The reader is concerned about her health and well-being and wants to improve it.

Now take the next step and brainstorm using this information to format queries. You could query *Woman's Day* on "Crushable Chic for Cruises," "Getting Stains Out Without Tears," "How to Display Your Dolls." Knowing the reader of any publication makes querying nearly foolproof.

9. Check the prose and how the articles are written. What's the sentence and paragraph length? What about buzz words? Do the articles use contractions, foreign words, and other specific ways that make the magazine unique. All this information will help you format a query that will sell.

10. Are the articles excerpts from books? Many publications use only book excerpts or previously published articles, as does *Reader's Digest*. If a magazine only uses reprints, even your best fresh stuff won't sell. However, some of your previously published articles might.

11. Draw a mental picture of this individual whom the editors and advertisers know well. If you submit an article to *Mature Living* about old grumpy oldsters in rocking chairs grumbling away their final years, trust me, it's unlikely to sell to any of the senior publications. However, if you're acquainted with their readers and query on seniors who volunteer in inner city schools, mall-walkers who assist the disabled, or a 78-year-old triathlete's training program, you could have a buyer.

Are there local or regional, ethnic, hobby, career, or age connections that must be included in your article to make it of interest to the editor and the reader? Why frustrate yourself if you query without these tie-ins. *Sunset* magazine, with a western focus and *only* sold in the West, accepts a small number of freelance writers. If you query *Sunset* about an article on skiing in the Alps, you've just wasted your time.

Making Money with This Information

Have you ever heard a writing instructor go on and on about how to analyze magazines in order to write just the right article? Recently I attended a seminar in another state and in one of workshops, the facilitator's topic sounded great: How to Make Money By Reading A Magazine.

I was all for it for about twenty minutes. Then this writing instructor began to tell us to list all of the types of articles used by the publications they want to query. He recommended a system that seemed more difficult than rewriting a phone book—and I'm not kidding. That's too much work for me and really leads to the same: The information needs to be gathered to write queries and sell articles.

Instead, do as successful writers do and brainstorm topics you think could be used in the magazines you've targeted. This brainstorming list will be the basis of queries and future articles. It's a valuable part of the writing process. You do not need to work out the ideas completely, yet by jotting down topics and the main thrust, you can return to the article idea when you have a few spare minutes.

Now check online or at the library to search if your topic for an article magazine has been published in the last two years. It has? Then put a spin on the focus and catch the editor's eye.

Keep in mind that the lead time (the time it takes to plan, research, assign, write and produce a magazine) varies from a few weeks, as with the tabloids, to six months or more for magazines like *Good Housekeeping* and *National Geographic*. If you're considering a timely or seasonal topic, find out that lead time. Sending in a Christmas cookie recipe in November, when the holidays are on your mind, will be far too late for this year's issue. You need to think Christmas in July and summer when you're dressed in a jacket, scarf and mittens.

Remember, too, ideas cannot be copyrighted. There may

be a staff or freelance writer *at this very moment* working on an article similar to your article's topic. It happens. The operative word here is *go*. Don't wait for inspiration or an act of nature. Get that query in the mail.

Cashing In on Trends

They're everywhere and trends keep successful writers busy with assigned articles to write. So where should you look for a scoop? News makes trends and anything can be news. Even old news is new when a twist or fad is added. Look at really skinny jeans, polyester, and platform shoes. And disco. For goodness' sake, did you ever really think all that would be back?

The busy writer who looks at trendy news happenings understands that people want to know more. Using the various formats such as how-to, informational and opinion articles, news and trends can make you money.

Because a magazine is planned and published weeks, even months, ahead of the date on the cover, those who write for periodicals work quickly. For example, there's a trend for cozy crafts, from weaving and stenciling, to crochet and collage. Anything made by loving hands (or doesn't look like it's been produced by machines) is hot. Those who write for home improvement magazines, women's magazines, and decorating publications are already submitting articles on this trend. Have you  noticed a trend and dismissed it? Think twice when you instinctively see lots of people getting into backyard gardening, cooking, or skydiving because you're probably seeing a trend in the making.

It's tough to predict or spot a new craze or fad. That's why beginners don't do it. The experienced writer takes information from sources such as scientific and medical journals, professional trade publications, and newspapers, and combines that data with economic forecasts and public opinion.

The information or experts quoted in these pieces can be the basis for an article in a popular magazine.

About fifteen years ago, people began to realize that a sedentary lifestyle could actually contribute to a number of health concerns. Couch potatoes ignored the advice, the rest of us sat up and began to work out. Magazines were starving for material because the public wanted it.

Remember the first sub-genre of how-to and self-help articles on high and low impact aerobics, target heart rate and heredity health risks? That "hot trend" is now an established sub-genre with scores of fitness and health magazines and is the end result of a "fad."

Take a minute to look at some trends that are worth writing about for the future. As baby boomers age, we can expect to read about and want to learn more (through magazine articles) about our health, retirement options, volunteering, and the grandparent/grandchild relationship. We'll want to know about sex after sixty and/or heart surgery, "salt-and-pepper" hairstyle options, wrinkle removal, and what to do with adult kids who move back into the deliciously empty nest.

What about topics like: second and entrepreneurial careers, managing the issues of aging parents, moving to smaller homes, buying and selling collectibles, purchasing vintage autos—anything that smacks of nostalgia of the '60s and '70s will sell. A savvy writer could have, on these topics alone, enough material to write for twenty years.

The environmental issues will continue to stay hot as will articles on child rearing. Pieces about recycling (including innovative uses of recycled materials such as in garden hoses and housing materials), and natural living appear on a regular basis in major magazines.

What is news? Anything that's of any interest to anyone. While there was once a standard format for all news articles, that's changed in recent years. Now articles often begin with quotes, bring in emotions, provide a slice of life in the first paragraph. To understand the new news format that's currently selling, study newspapers such as the *Wall Street Journal* and *USA Today*. The material is still concise, sentences are short, and now the text is entertaining as well as informative. Sidebars are often included.

The rookie queries magazines for an article on a news item just as the occurrence happens. Then after dashing off the query, wonders why he or she is turned down on a news-oriented article. The veteran writer combines news with one of the formats for popular article styles mentioned above and sells the article.

Since the lead time for the production of a magazine article is longer than a newspapers, real events such as wild fires in San Diego County or monster floods in the Midwest would be of little interest if a magazine publishes it months after the last ember has been snuffed out or the final mop-and-bucket crew has finished. That's exactly why the beginner's articles on these news topics are turned down flat. News sells articles, but they must reflect a timeless aspect if they are to be used by magazines.

You are not a news reporter, use a slant

Now if that freelance writer interviews burned-out homeowners who have become the owner/builder as they construct their dream homes on the once-scorched earth, that's an article. If the freelancer talks with officials about crisis intervention for the town's kids who saw homes, pets, and people wash away, that's an article. Use the news you read today to build articles that are timeless and have universal appeal.

Of course, you could hire a psychic to predict what will happen in the future so that your article queries are on target, or you could begin today to watch buying trends, and stay abreast of cultural interests.

'Tis Always the Season for Seasonal Material

In reviewing *Writer's Digest* and *Writer* and other magazines, look at magazines that buy seasonal material. The submittal requirements for seasonal material are often a number of months before the article is to be published.

New writers think of the traditional, basic four seasons, plus Christmas and Hanukkah. When they do, they miss out on article potential because seasonal means more. What about the season that desert cacti bloom? The winter recreational options for the "snowbirds" who flock to Palm Springs and Phoenix? September back-to-school clothing necessities?

Check out "other" holidays like Statehood Day, Columbus Day, Martin Luther King's birthday, Arbor Day, National Pet Care Week, Volunteers-Are-Important Month, or Let's Celebrate Pittsburgh Day. Take a look at *Chase's Annual Events*, a reference book that lists every event you can imagine and scores of others. Magazines want seasonal material and specializing in this area could pay well and build your reputation.

Locating "Other" Magazines

As I mentioned in the beginning, there are scores of magazines that could use you as a writer and pay for your writing, but you'll never find these magazines on the bookstore or grocery market shelf. Here's the rundown to get you started locating the "other" magazines.

Trade Journals

Professional magazines that focus on a specific career or industry are called trade magazines and trade journals. Organizations and companies publish magazines on everything from *Auto Glass Journal* and *Fur Trade Journal of Canada* to *Supervision* and *Form & Function*.

Writer's Digest lists over six hundred different trade publications, as do other writer's sources. The magazines are specifically addressed to a certain segment of the working world and could be gold for the capable writer.

The Standard Rate and Data Service publishes *The Business Publication Volume. Gale's Directory of Publications and Broadcast Media*, and *Gebbie Press All-In-One Directory*. These and others are excellent sources to ferret out trade magazines, especially if you're looking for new ones. It's been determined that about half of the trade publications buy freelance material. You can write for writer's guidelines, call and ask the magazine's receptionist, or write a letter asking if they will accept queries. Beginners rarely get this far; freelance writers go the distance, and match query ideas with the magazine's special readership.

A good example of this is a magazine targeted specifically at professional golf course maintenance personnel. For a few years, I was on staff at one of these trade magazines. I learned a whole lot about turf grass and problems associated with maintenance of tournament greens.

This trade magazine, published in San Diego, is mailed free of charge to groundskeepers and golf course designers throughout the country. It's not listed in the usual writer's reference sources. I found it by chance when I was stalking the shelves of used magazines at a library sale. I contacted the editor. She was polite but not too encouraging, yet she did ask me to submit some samples of my work. I did the next day and within a week, had an interview and a half dozen freelance assignments. No, I never became an expert on grass types or problems, but I turned out interviews with experts in the field, trends, and fast-breaking stories on everything from seed to fungus diseases that can affect lawn growth.

What separates you from the rest and increases your profit is that you're willing to go the extra distance to find writing work. To find trade magazines, talk with friends, ask associates,  chat with those in service fields about specific magazines for their industry. You'll find that 99 percent of professionals love to talk about their trade and will inundate you with "their" magazine. Ask them to save back issues of trade magazines, ask that their spouse's bring them home, too.

Review the magazines closely including format, style, terms and length. Format a query along with a self-addressed stamped envelope (SASE), offer your services as a cracker jack interviewer (if you are) and get that letter in the mail *now*.

Local and Other Magazines

Local magazines, such as one published by your Chamber of Commerce, hold great selling possibilities. These are also the magazines sent by your insurance agent, and ones found on the counter of the health food store. As a wise magazine writer, you will no longer consider these freebies to be junk.

The beginner does not pick them up to read while waiting for the clerk to total his or her purchase. The beginner snubs the publication and thinks, "Why everybody knows these magazines are junk—free for the taking and thus worthless to a *real* writer." This beginner assumes the magazines don't pay or pay much for freelance work and only contacts those trade or consumer magazines listed in established reference books.

Let's be glad there are beginners like this. It increases our success in selling to other magazines. Why? The experienced magazine writer clings to anything that looks like it could produce a possibility for a sale. With that free magazine in hand, review the masthead (the listing of editors, writers, publishers usually found in the first few pages of the magazine).

Don't be surprised if the "local" magazine in your St. Paul, Minnesota hardware store is published in Fort Lauderdale, Florida. Some local magazines only look local. They are produced by a national organization that distributes to stores, shops and suppliers across the nation. Local merchants pay for their name to appear either as advertising inside or in a way that looks like they're publishing the magazine. These magazines, the freebies, and the tabloid types are well worth time and attention (and a query) for the experienced writer who is determined to make a good living at his or her trade.

Weekly Newspapers and News Magazines

Even though the book title states how-to write for magazines, a discussion of writing for weekly newspapers needs to be included. They provide news and buy newsy articles. They also use feature articles, how-to pieces, millions of interviews, columns and consumer information pieces. They are regularly ignored by the beginner because, "Why, that's a newspaper. I'm not a reporter—I'm a magazine writer!"

Granted the pay may not be stupendous, because weekly papers serve a limited area, yet you may be able to sell the same features throughout the country to these smaller markets. Multiply that payment of $10.00 by 1000 weekly newspapers and they suddenly have a serious edge.

You'll find weekly newspapers listed in *Gale's Directory of Publications and Broadcast Media* and *Gebbie Press All-In-One Directory*. Most large public libraries and university libraries own copies of these and other reference books. If you live in a small town, don't let that stop you since librarians are always helpful to serious writers, some are on-line.

Ethnic Magazines

Gale's Directory of Publications and Broadcast Media and *Gebbie Press All-In-One Directory* can also provide you with publications directed to minority readers. This is a vast and profitable market.

The beginner may falsely think because he or she isn't of a certain race, religion, or ethnic background, it's impossible to write for an ethnic magazine. The experienced writer knows good copy transcends boundaries. Contact ethnic magazines, query ethnic magazines, write for them again and again.

Association and Corporate Newsletters

Does the company where you do your "day job" have a newsletter? What about the company for which your significant other works? Most companies, corporations, groups, and non-profit organizations have newsletters. And they're often looking for articles.

Depending on your focus, newsletters provide exposure, give you clips (published article samples) and help you polish your writing skills. Many newsletters pay for articles.

Interested? Find the editor's phone number or address, get more information, and query.

International Publications

As with ethnic magazines, you needn't speak Japanese to write for a Tokyo-based magazine. That's a beginner's mind set. International publications, the flight magazines, those geared to foreign residents and visitors buy and regularly pay freelancers for articles.

The international markets are an excellent source for reprints of your articles, previously sold in the United States, unless you have sold all rights of course. When sending an article to a foreign periodical, it's professional to explain that your article originally appeared in such and such magazine.

With international markets, unless they specifically request it, it's not necessary to include money for return postage. Somehow that's only an American custom. Also, you may have to request that funds be transmitted to you in US dollars. A few will subtract their national income tax from the payment. And most are exceedingly happy and pay promptly to use American writers' material.

Columns

Every magazine and newspaper you can mention has columns. Some follow the how-to format, others use opinion pieces. Some require humor, reviews, and critiques.

Often the columns are open to freelance writers. You must, of course, find out which newspapers and magazines use freelance work—that only requires a phone call or letter (with SASE).

The novice who wants to write columns sends a sample column to one of the big name magazines or syndicates, such as King Features, and waits for a positive reply. He or she never assesses the market, never bothers to query the syndicate, never considers that using "the back door", i.e., making his or her name known and the material wanted before approaching the syndicate, might be the best method.

A proficient freelancer asks for and reads the writer's guidelines or information in writer's marketing books. Depending on the magazine or paper and the type of column, a query may be appropriate. For example, I wrote a column for the "Psychology" department of *Dance Exercise Today*, a trade journal specifically for those who teach aerobic dance exercise. "Psychology" is a regular feature, and the editor uses both lay writers and experts who report on various topics each month. A query was appropriate and it sold the piece.

For the last 20 years, I've collaborated on a regular column with a internationally known fitness expert. The column is read worldwide. In the beginning, we wrote four sample columns and sent them to a syndicate, giving the editors the option of trying the columns out "without obligation." The response was positive and the rest is history. Yes, we had to give four columns away, but that was years ago and the column is still going strong. I often see my articles "picked up" by women's magazines, local and regional publications as well as the local paper. I recently gave permission for a reprint in a university magazine.

King Features, United Press International, and the other big-name syndicates are flooded with queries and sample columns. If you have material that is special or unique, be prepared to market the column yourself. Write the column for your local paper or magazine. When they become addicted, offer it to other "local" papers and publications. Build from there to other markets, and then present your concept to the top-notch syndication company.

Advertorials

Advertorials are a marriage between advertising copy and editorial copy, thus the name. Advertorials are found in scores of publications. They are the special advertising sections that look like articles, but end up attempting to sell products or services. On a closer-to-home scale, they're often submitted to local newspapers by community professionals. In my local papers, there's an advertorial by a chiropractor, an attorney, and a make-up expert. The articles give advice on the experts' specialties and then give the address and phone number so that consumers, who want to pay for more information, can do so.

If your local papers run advertorials, if you want to write copy for a big company, then ask. Back up your question with samples of your work, possibly do some writing on spec and then get ready to write for money.

Small and Non-Paying Markets

While this book stresses writing for money, don't ever consider yourself less of a writer if you submit work to publications that pay in copies only. When starting out or changing your genre, there may be times when it's more important to establish yourself as a writer and get a byline (and the clip) than get the cash. This is also true when you really want your message to get into the hands of the right reader, then a small magazine, which may or may not pay writers. Then it's the right choice. I recently wrote an article for a writer's magazine about publications that pay in copies (and not in currency). Every magazine editor I interviewed was supportive, energetic, helpful and pleased to work with new writers.

If I were starting out again and needed published clips of my work, you can bet I would submit work to a small or non-paying market. The choice is yours—it's your career in the making.

Collaborating—Double Your Sales

Some writers approach the concept of collaboration from two standpoints. Either they're afraid of it and refuse to collaborate because working with another writer indicates they're new to magazine writing *or* they are scared that the other writer will steal their golden words.

Experienced writers see huge potential (read that profits) in writing with a collaborator, especially if one partner is an expert, has an advanced degree, or has accomplished something noteworthy. Often magazine articles are ghostwritten for the expert, and in that case the writer's name would not appear on the article.

With "as told to" articles, collaboration is understood. Informational articles are often joint projects, and experienced writers know that an expert's name on the article query will multiply the chances for the article idea to be sold.

With any partnership, good contracts are essential. Talk with your attorney, a literary agent (if you have one you probably write books, too), someone at your writer's organization or other writers about their partnership and collaboration agreement. Draw up a letter agreement itemizing your individual and joint responsibilities, exactly who does what and when, including how profits will be shared. You'll want to outline how expenses will be handled. If your partner is responsible for the research, can he or she deduct the cost of gasoline to and from the library out of the profit from the sale of the article?

Writing partnerships are like marriages, without love. Work out the pre-writing terms and then be willing to compromise. Many find that two writers work better and help motivate each other. Before you say "No thanks," look over the article idea and be open to the possibilities for the published article helping your own career.

CHIN UP
AND ALL THAT

F reelance writing can be a lonely profession. It can isolate us. When researching, searching, or returning books to the library, I often meet a man who freelances for a military magazines. Granted, he might have a somber personality, but he seems desperate for conversation. It doesn't have to be this way. My acquaintance and freelancers who feel isolated need to look beyond their home office for motivation.

Here are some tips on keeping your energy high:

- Maintain a list or file of the good things that happen to you as a writer. For example, when you receive a thank you note from an editor for a job well done, pin it to your bulletin board or place it in your "Smile File" for days when all might not be rosy.

- When you are complimented on your writing talent, physically stop, concentrate on the emotion you're feeling, and relish the sense of satisfaction. Use this technique when you accomplish something difficult, perhaps calling an editor with (what you think is) the scoop of the century, or doing your first interview, or completing a complicated computer class.

- Join a writer's group and a national organization, such as the National Writers Association, in Aurora, Colorado.

- Take advanced writing classes. Attend a meeting or two to make sure if you like the philosophy, schedule and structure.

- Attend at least two writing conferences each year, more if you can afford the fee and/or the time commitment.

- Subscribe to some writing magazines, such as *The Writer* and *Writer's Digest*, or read them at the library. Most of the articles are written for beginners; however, I always find a "gee whiz" bit of information.

- Join a book club and read books on creativity and writing. This is your business and even an experienced writer can learn.

- Form your own writer's network. Be warned, some informal writers' groups turn out to be gripe sessions. Who needs that energy?

- Make copies of your published articles and clips. Keep them ready to send out with future queries.

- Offer to teach a free writing class at the library, high school, senior center or college—or organize one for a fee.

- Update your resume. Nothing helps inflate an ego like listing all the articles you've written, all the magazines that have printed your work, and all the topics on which you're qualified to write.

• Frame the original or a photocopy of some of your most eloquent articles. Hang them in your office like post-graduate degrees.

Extra Sparks to Fire Up Your Work

If you have yet to make a commitment to buy letterhead, envelopes and business cards imprinted with your name, etc., chances for success could be trimmed. As with any business, the more professional you appear, the more confidence others will have in your business. Many software programs and office supply stores carry everything you need to set up a business image. The big copy store can also provide a service. Shop around for the best buys.

A sentence included in your query that photos, illustrations, and expert interviews are included in the article you're querying will not guarantee that a magazine editor will snap up your idea. Yet if a magazine regularly uses them, it could mean the difference between a sale and a rejection. Why do beginners neglect this facet of sales? Because it takes some extra work that becomes routine for experienced writers.

On illustrations or photos, you must ask and perhaps pay for their use. However, you needn't pay until you have a confirmed assignment from a magazine. Some magazines will reimburse you for the expense or pay for the photo or illustration. (Note: Some magazines use their own photographers or illustrators.)

Here is how to get the illustrations you want and need:

1. Take the photos or do the illustration yourself. Obviously, you have to have talent in the field. Don't say that you'll include professional photographs if you can't provide them.

2. Contact a commercial photographer or illustrator. See if he or she will take the photo or produce an illustration when you get the article assignment. If art payments aren't listed in the magazine's guidelines, ask. Often you can work

with a photographic student who is eager to make a name for him or herself and will do an excellent and enthusiastic job. A student will likely charge less, but don't expect to pay slave wages. You're a professional.

3. Stock photo agencies supply photos to magazine writers and are listed in the yellow pages of the phone book under Photographs-Stock Shots. Tell them what you have in mind and see if they have a photo in stock which will illustrate your article. They charge for this service.

4. This is my absolute favorite, but it depends on the subject of your article. There are hundreds of associations that support various causes which will supply photos. Manufacturing companies would be happy to have their product appear in a magazine. It's free exposure. Normally they have to pay for the type of editorial coverage you're offering. You'll can get names of companies, addresses and phone numbers from the reference books at the library.

When submitting the article, illustrations, and photos, remember to give credit, make sure all material is returned (if it's needed), and stay in good graces. You may need the company, group or association again when you rewrite the article for a non-competing magazine.

Why go to all this trouble? Our beginner wouldn't bother. But as an experienced writer, you know that offering illustrations or photographs to accompany your article, if appropriate, will triple your chances of an assignment to write the piece.

Here's a sample interview and photo release I've used. Why use them? So that the person you interview or photograph knows exactly what you plan to do with the interview or likeness and whether you're planning to pay. The magazine you're working with might have its own specific form.

I keep a form of each of the following (inserting the correct description) in a file on my hard drive. There's no need to recreate it every time I need the form.

Interview (Photo) Release

I, _____ (interviewee or photo subject's name inserted here), give my permission to (your name and/or the magazine) to use my interview (photograph) in conjunction with (article name). I understand that no payment is expected for the use of the interview (or photo). I do (or do not) wish to review the interview before the magazine article is submitted to the editor.

_____   _____
Signature   Date

Getting an Expert's Opinion

There's plenty of discussion when magazine writers get together on the topic of when to contact experts for quotes, information or opinions. I think it depends. Not too long ago, I queried *Living Fit* on the subject of journaling as a weight management technique. Before sending the query, I contacted Sheila Cluff, a nationally known health and fitness expert, and I talked with a few psychologists on journaling techniques for those patients in addiction recovery. Everyone I spoke with and told about my article idea said basically the same thing: "Sure, I'd be happy to be interviewed for the article, when the time comes." I used that information in my query. I got the assignment.

Conducting a lengthy interview without an assignment might waste your time and your expert's time, too. It's best to be honest with the expert as to how much time you'll need, and how much time for an interview when you get the assignment. In your query, use a statement such as "Many experts in the field of (what you're writing about) will be interviewed for their important (controversial, notable, provocative, intriguing, educated) opinions."

Joining a Group and Learning From the Pros

It used to be that critique or writer's groups were only for fiction writers. That changed for the better and now there are groups for people like us—who write commercial nonfiction magazine articles. To find one, check with one of the national writers' organizations for a local branch, or ask at the community college or bookstore about writers groups. (Sometimes bookstores and coffee houses sponsor writers' groups.) Your local librarian might be a good resource, too. Or organize a group yourself.

Every group has its own personality. Make sure you are comfortable with the type of critique offered, the group dynamics, meeting times, etc. Visit before you become a member.

You can also learn a lot from the pros, without ever leaving your office.

Like many of you, every year I make career resolutions. One that I've kept is to read more and often about my profession: Writing. I've become addicted to writing books and also subscribe to various writers' magazines. Take a hint and read the newest and oldest books on writing. I study creativity as if my future depended on it—and it does!

At least 15 minutes a day. Good news... reading this book counts

Take your craft seriously and become earnest on improving your writing and creative skills. Have you read Julia Cameron's *The Artist's Way*? What about *The Courage to Write* by Bruce Keyes? You're missing some great stuff. See Appendix A for other books on creativity, writing and writers; learn from the pros.

Now's the time to take self-improvement classes, too, whether you're looking to improve your computer skills or your public speaking abilities. Don't forget to include time to exercise, stretch, and feel good about yourself. The more personal confidence you have, the better your writing will be.

Check out the classes offered through your community college and/or the extension of the university in your area. Good classes, usually taught by working writers, are at prices you'll want to afford.

In a more professional arena, make sure you attend at least one or two writing conferences every year. If you haven't been to a writers' conference, put it on your "must do" list. They come in all price ranges, and listings can be found in writers' magazines and some of the writers' reference books. Your local library will probably have a May issue of *Writer's Digest*. It lists many of the conferences, state by state; call your local college about conferences they sponsor, too.

Look for specialty conferences, such as those for science writers, children's writers, craft writers, Christian writers, food and cooking writers. Ask other writing friends about the conferences they've attended. Did they get their money's worth? Were there classes, read and critique sessions, or only lectures? Were they able to mingle with published writers, editors, and agents?

Before going, do your "homework." Look over the agenda when you receive the conference brochure. Can you submit manuscripts? Will there be critique groups? Lectures? Networking times? Do local hotels give discounts? Find out which magazine editors (or book publishers) will be at the conference and write them a note. Why? You'll make a connection in the least; at the most, you'll get your foot in that magazine's door.

At any conference, be ready to "pitch" ideas, that is to provide a verbal query to an editor. If the editor is interested, follow with a written query or confirmation letter when you get back to your office.

While you're there to chat with fellow writers and editors, you'll also learn from listening. Steer clear of attendees who just want to protest the sad state of publishing and how terrible it is to write for magazines. It's easy to get pulled into negativity. Rather network with other writers in your genre. It's comforting to know that there are other people with your same goals and desires who have lived through rejection, too.

Finding the Time to Write

You're working at home. You can make your own hours and come and go as you please. And, as a frustrated, candid novice may tell you, it's very easy to waste time. That's what happens to some beginners—they have so much freedom that they sideline success.

Or allow others to do it for them

Use whatever means necessary to budget time. You might want to start with working during set hours of the day, say from eight to noon. Depending on your writing assignments, research or collaborative work, four hours may not be enough. Set up a regular office routine and be realistic.

If you're a morning person or a night person, understand your personal limitations, but don't use them as an excuse for not writing. Should you find twenty different reasons why you can't write (i.e., kids coming in and out, the laundry has to be done, a friend needs a visit, etc.), review your goals and objectives. There's absolutely nothing wrong with putting your writing career on hold until you are able to concentrate or have some discretionary time.

As with any profession, you'll have good days and not-so-good days, but with magazine writing, there's always something to do from developing article ideas to organizing your office. On good days, write like crazy. On the other ones, run errands, network. Research future topics.

The bottom line here is that if you don't write queries, submit articles, rewrite manuscripts, and continue to pursue your career, you won't get paid or build a reputation as a magazine writer.

I'm often asked how much time I put in writing each

day—to be truthful it varies. Usually, it's a minimum of eight hours, sometimes more, often on weekends. About half of that time is spent marketing my work, from writing queries and talking to editors to researching new markets and selling myself to seminar chairpersons.

I also teach writing classes through the extension programs at the University of California, consult and write for ghostwriting clients, and speak at workshops and seminars.

Of course, I'm obsessed with writing; I love it, and I'm fast at it too. That makes the end result (getting paid for doing something I enjoy) even finer.

Not everyone is committed or has the determination to be a writer. If your problems center around organization and time management, read up on the topic and practice what you read. From time to time we can all use a booster shot of organization skills to get back on track again.

Facing Writer's Block

What is Writer's Block? Is it a hoax perpetuated by those hounding the pages of a dictionary for just the right word? Is it an excuse for those who talk about writing—and only talk? Is it a creative recess necessary to produce ingenious thoughts? Is it produced through stress and exhaustion? Can it be cured?

Whether it's real or imaginary and whether you really suffer with it or think it's baloney, it is a topic for discussion. I believe the best way to deal with writer's block is to give a good hard look. It's ludicrous to think of your dentist, dry cleaner, or the individual who operates the photo store around the corner waiting until the mood strikes to attend to a customer or complete a task. That said, remember there are times when other things are going on, and you simply do not feel creative.

For most magazine writers, there are no bolts of lightning or messages from beyond on how to construct an articulate

sentence or to keep a reader on the edge of a chair. If words don't come, you're probably tired, stressed, overworked, anxious and/or a string of other real problems. Writer's block is only fatal to novice writers; the rest of us find ways to get over it.

Here are some suggestions:

- Get out of the office or your home for an hour.

- Take a walk. Exercise often helps unravel knotty problems. Then get back to work on that project or another one on which you are working.

- Begin a different writing project or another section of the same article. Sometimes hooks are impossible to "get right." Smart writers work on another segment of an article until the words begin to flow, then return to write or rewrite that first paragraph or problem area.

- Go to the library for research; your block may be caused from not having sufficient material.

- Reread or retype material you've already written to improve it.

- Write thank you letters to editors, friends, networking contacts.

- Contact new or perspective magazine editors.

- Make lists of what's needed to complete this project.

- Update your query file.

- Use the bubble method to put new twists on old article ideas.

- Organize your office and materials.

- Have a quick chat with another writer discussing your current problem.

- Get a non-writer's input.

- Seek out and analyze one new source for your

work by looking through some writer's market guides.

- Do anything that helps your writing, so that your "boss" (that is, you) doesn't know you're stumbling.

(Note: These suggestions do not include excessive eating, drinking, lunching, tv-watching, or any other "ing" or activity not *directly* related to your current project.)

42 Ways to Make It as a Writer

Writing is a business. Your business. And remember:

1. Believe in yourself first.
2. Develop and maintain a positive attitude.
3. Set and achieve goals.
4. Learn the fundamentals and continue to practice them.
5. Write what you know about.
6. Continue to learn, take classes, buy teaching books, and study your industry as if your future depends on it.
7. Visualize the sale of articles and books.
8. Shake hands firmly.
9. Be conversational in your business dealings.
10. Be great on the telephone.
11. Understand your customers and their needs.
12. Take notes about prospective customers.
13. Sell your services to help others.
14. Be prepared. Always.
15. Become a resource for others and your customers.
16. Look professional.
17. Be prompt.
18. Do what you say and say what you'll do.

19. Establish rapport and confidence.

20. Understand the power of the question.

21. Deliver—and over deliver.

22. Realize objections before they are voiced.

23. Tell the truth.

24. Don't put down the competition.

25. Follow up, follow up, follow up.

26. Follow the rules.

27. Treat others as you'd like to be treated.

28. Trust people.

29. Don't blame others when it's your fault.

30. Understand that hard work makes luck.

31. Develop and practice networking skills.

32. Evaluate yourself every month.

33. Make it easy to do business with you.

34. Don't keep score.

35. Don't do anything that wouldn't make your mom proud.

36. Keep fit, stay trim.

37. Be memorable.

38. Find mentors (you can have more than one) and use them.

39. Hang around successful people.

40. Realize the biggest obstacle to your success is you.

41. Smile—even at times when you least feel like it.

42. Have fun; create the life you want to live.

Treating Yourself Like An Expert

What do you really need to succeed? A plush, expensive office? A fancy new computer system with a Pentium chip? A personal assistant/secretary? A beginner insists he or she must have this and that before writing a query. An experienced writer knows that tenacity along with a typewriter or word processor and his or her brain, paper, envelopes and stamps are the only requirements for success.

Don't let what you do not own or possess stand in the way of your success. If you need excuses, you can find plenty, from needing to get the oil changed on the car to finishing a degree. Using excuses is a beginner's mindset, and then the novice wonders why there are never any acceptance letters in that mailbox.

Treat yourself like an expert. Tell people you're a magazine writer. Answer the phone during working hours like a professional. Join professional organizations. Dress for success when talking to editors and the experts you interview.

Begin to assemble the tools of your profession from a dictionary to a small tape recorder. If money is a consideration, budget and barter. You don't need everything right away.

For the first article I ever sold, I was paid $54 and it felt like a million bucks. Do you remember your first sale? Back then I wrote on a manual Smith Corona and used the dining room table for a desk. My office was a cardboard box I could move out of the dining room when the family demanded to eat dinner.

After hearing that my article had been accepted, I hung up the phone and screamed for joy. I could prove I was a "real" writer when my first by-lined article appeared. With the puny, and greatly appreciated amount of money, I paid an electric bill (this was years ago) and had just enough left over to buy a new dictionary. Today, I sit in my home office, check spelling with fancy software and contact writers and editors via e-mail (connected to a dedicated phone line). And Old Webster? The book still has a place in my heart, and I keep it close to remember the feel of that first sale. Bottom line? Don't forget your "roots," and take pride in your progress as a successful writer.

THE NUTS AND BOLTS OF A SUCCESSFUL WRITER

T itles hook your reader and a good title is your opportunity to sell the piece or at least to nudge it closer to a sale. A mundane or (gasp!) lackluster title won't prevent a sale, although a great title can add sizzle and quite possibly make the sale.

Title Your Work—"Name the Baby"

Some writers become "title collectors." While not thinking about any article's content, they keep a list or computer file on potentially prize-winning titles. Other writers play the word game of "Let's Name This Article," and the more they do it, the better they become.

Here are some title tips to remember:

  1. Titles are labels, headlines and calling cards.

2. Too often, editors and magazine readers *only* read titles before selecting what to read.
3. Key phrases, lists (i.e., "Ten Ways to—"), snappy word twists, provocative questions can become titles.
4. A title, like an idea, cannot be copyrighted.
5. Sometimes the title just doesn't "happen," but once the article is complete, it appears like a lightning bolt or whispers like a hummingbird in flight.
6. Come up with several titles. Say them out loud. If your tongue can't make it through a title, an editor's won't either.

Here's a list of various title categories:

How-to titles

Rhyming titles

Frightening titles

Shock titles

Trick titles

Silly titles

Question titles

Short titles

Punch-line titles

List titles

Item titles

Statistic titles

Can't sell an article or query? Just retitle it.

Power Words Advertisers Do Not Want You to Know

Advertising and sales is an art form and big business. Smart freelancers know the "power words" that people in advertising use to make consumers want to buy. Why not use the words (when appropriate) to add gusto to queries and articles? Here's the list:

you	free	imagine	it's here
modern	switch	go	powerful
just	sale	how to	advantage
why	learn	save	just arrived
quick	latest	what	high-tech
unique	deserve	fast	introducing
do	easy	new	revolutionary
proven	built	idea	dramatically
call	great	first	last chance
visit	success	bargain	breakthrough

Write That Hook and Keep It Alive

The "hook," lead or thesis is what draws your reader into the article. If it's dull, don't waste the postage.

A quote, a question, a comparison, a statistic are all good ways to lead into an article. I like using an anecdote and then using part of the anecdote at the end. (Remember, not all anecdotes are funny.)

The hook starts strong, and also foretells what you're about to present. Some writers use any first sentence that comes to mind when they write the first draft. When the article is finished and they know how it ends, then they go back and write the hook.

Now keep the interest going. Contemporary magazine articles are quick to read and easy to understand. As you look over the sample copies of those you want to write for, check out the writing style. *Family Circle*, for instance, uses lots of list articles, i.e., "10 Ways to Decorate on a Budget." Other magazines use lots of quotes, statistics, or examples.

Focus on three to ten subtopics for the middle section of your article, depending on the depth of your topic. Keep the reader's interest by supplying enough details so he or she feels satisfied, but not bloated with information, and again make your writing reflect the style of the magazine in which it will be published.

Now let's look at the end. Today's articles end quickly—just look at any popular magazine. The article's writer provides information, makes a point, and leaves the reader. Words to the wise: *Don't overkill the end. Keep it simple.*

Writing the Sidebar

Sidebars are the boxed, smaller articles that are included with larger articles. Most popular magazines use sidebars, some use two per article.

When querying an article or writing it, think sidebar material. I often save an integral item of the article, that supports the topic, for a sidebar. For instance, if I were writing "How to Choose the Right Cat for Your Family," I might have a sidebar on "Kitten-Proofing a Home," or one on "Creative Litter Box Solutions."

Don't draw a box around the text to indicate sidebars. Rather indicate that you're using a sidebar this way: [Sidebar Begins]. Write your sidebar in the normal manuscript format, then indicate the end with [Sidebar Ends].

How to Self-Edit

I've heard of a time years ago before I became a full-time writer when editors helped magazine writers "clean up" and polish an article. Not any more. It's up to us to send in polished work. A typo here and a missed word there, notwithstanding, every writer should self-edit.

Words of warning about having someone close to you critique your writing or the article. This takes two special people, and I don't recommend allowing your spouse or significant other to critique your work. Instead ask another writer you admire to read an article. Or put the article away for a week, then review it as your own critic. I ruthlessly edit my work—with a red pen—and evaluate it from a reader's standpoint.

What to look for? Redundancy. If you've said or inferred anything twice, trim out one of them. If you're using a memorable or descriptive word more than once, get creative. Trim out the extras. If you abuse modifiers (very, really, etc.) or other words such as "that," cut, cut, cut. With any interviews in your articles, trim redundancy by paraphrasing your expert, but make sure you're still saying what the expert meant to say.

There's an old adage in creative writing classes that if a fiction writer's story describes a musket hanging over the fireplace, it better darn well be fired before that story ends. Or it doesn't belong in your article. Check for "muskets."

The Acid Test

As any writer knows, feedback is essential. We get it when our work is accepted; we get it with rejection slips.

Before sending out your next project (query, finished article, column, book proposal or book), give it the "acid test." Be fair with your self-evaluation. If you become frustrated as to why a piece isn't selling, put it through the test, too.

Give each "Yes" answer 10 points.
Give each "No" answer 0.

_____ 1. Does the lead have a strong first sentence or paragraph?

_____ 2. Does the hook snag the reader's attention?

_____ 3. Does the article make a promise?

_____ 4. Does the article fulfill the promise indicated in the hook?

_____ 5. Does the middle hold possibilities?

_____ 6. Is your main theme reflected throughout the article?

_____ 7. Could each paragraph stand alone?

_____ 8. Is your slant clear?

_____ 9. Is the big picture covered, too?

_____ 10. Does each paragraph have a topic sentence?

_____ 11. Do all sentences support the paragraph's topic sentence?

_____ 12. Have you stated the topic sentence only once?

_____ 13. Are quotes pertinent? Do they substantiate the topic sentence?

_____ 14. Are statistics accurate and do they contribute?

_____ 15. Are the examples applicable?

_____ 16. Do the anecdotes further the premise?

_____ 17. Does your article provide a service?

_____ 18. Does it entertain, inform, incite, or expose something?

_____ 19. Does your article give enough information that your reader can really do what you've outlined?

_____ 20. Can you state five ways that the piece helps/informs a reader?

_____ 21. Have you double checked spelling/grammar in your article?

_____ 22. Check word count if applicable?

_____ 23. Is it neat and attractively presented?

_____ 24. Did you wind everything up, possibly with a punch?

_____ 25. If you were a first-time reader, would you enjoy it?

_____ 26. Are you satisfied with what you've written?

Scoring:

250-200:	Send it out;
195-150:	Make topic sentences and the hook fulfill their promises;
145-90:	Let it "cool" for a week and get back to it with renewed enthusiasm;
under 85:	Do more research, give it a twist, take a totally new approach and return to the Bubble Method to focus on marketable ideas.

The Must-Do Final Step

Typos are like garden snails. They seem to sneak in, regardless of how careful you are and do damage. Before the final printing of your article, run it through your computer's spell check one more time. So you remember that word processing programs produce perfect words, here's a little poem, author unknown:

My Spell Checker

I have a little spell checker,
It came with my PC.
It plainly marks for my revue,
mistakes I cannot sea.
I've run this poem threw it,
I'm sure your please too no.
It's letter perfect and its write,
My checker tolled me sew.

Ten 10

MONEY TALKS

Want to write for *Sky & Telescope?* You can expect to be paid between 15 cents to 25 cents per word. Writing articles that would be perfect for *Evangel*, the rate is 4 cents a word. On the other end of the scale, *American Health, Eating Well, Esquire, Ladies' Home Journal, New York, Rolling Stone, Playboy*, and *TV Guide* are in the $3,500 per article ballpark range.

There is no set dollar figure for writing an article; every magazine is different. Some pay by the word, from five cents to $10. Some pay a set amount for all articles within a general word length. Some pay more if you're a writer with a postgraduate degree or a degree in a specific field, such as medicine. Some pay more if you've published with them before.

Writer's Market and *The Writer's Handbook*, published annually, often include fees for writing services. Within the detailed listings per magazine category, the rates are given at the time the book was published. Things change as to the rates magazines pay writers. Ask for writer's guidelines before or when you query a magazine. Find out, beforehand, what you can expect to be paid for your work. Also realize that depending on your background and experience (or the desirability of an article), it could be possible to negotiate a higher rate than shown in *Writer's Market* or *The Writer's Handbook*. Don't be shy—ask about being paid for expenses such as telephone calls, travel and mileage, or costs incurred by taking the expert of your interview article out to dinner.

What can you expect when writing on spec or assignment? It's a "given" that magazines make money when people buy the magazines they've produced. As a writer, the articles you provide satisfy the magazine's consumers' needs.

The consumer buys the magazine for the editorial content and sometimes the advertising, such as with *Arts and Activities*, and *Glamour*. The advertising and the cover price pay for the cost of production and your services as a writer.

Novice writers believe, at times, that magazines will steal their work. Some seasoned writers think this too. But it's not so. Magazine editors need good writers—that's you. Yet, just like with any business, things can go wrong. The system can hiccup and your query may be misplaced. Your job as a writer is to make sure you know where your articles ideas are, when articles are to be printed, and when you should be paid.

Working on an assigned article means that the editor is eager for your talent and is counting on your ability to meet a deadline. If you don't produce the article that's expected (or it's not up to the quality desired) there will be a hole in the issue. Not a good thing, by any means. The editor is planning to use the article and counting on you to come through. It feels good to be on assignment. Some writers won't work any other way.

When you write an article on assignment, should it not be used for any reason, you should receive a kill fee. A kill fee is normally about half of what would have been paid had the article been used. Typically the copyrights are returned to you, but you might have to write for them. Then you can resell the article or a spin-off, depending on your contract with the magazine's editor.

Don't be turned off by being asked to write an article on speculation (often called "spec"). This may be the only way you'll get your foot into this magazine's door. Everybody prefers to write articles with a definite assignment and some refuse to go a step further. I don't let the word spec scare me. And taking calculated chances with editors has been profitable.

Be aware that an article asked for on spec is written without any promises for publication. You can look at writing on spec as negative or as a challenge with incredible results. When I began writing for magazines, I knew the articles I wrote were a cut above the competition. I'd studied each market and understood the language and techniques used by the magazines I wanted to write for. I decided early on to take chances. The chances paid off because if I really wanted to be considered for future assignments, I had to write on spec. Sure I failed—I'd be lying if I tried to tell you otherwise. But for the most part, say 85 percent of the time, I hit the mark in the form of a sale and regular assignments from magazines.

Nowadays, I'd rather work on assignment, but after an editor has shown specific and perhaps personal interest in my query, I know that I'll write on spec. The odds are that good for me and they can be for you too.

They Are Your Rights—Possibly

In order to make more money, know your rights—publication rights, that is. There are a number of reference books which provide complete explanations of various publication rights. (See the book list at the end.)

Most often, you will be asked to sell *all copyrights*, including electronic rights. This means that the magazine's publisher may use the article because you've been paid for your work.

You may not resell the article in that form or a form closely resembling the original.

While that might seem that all is lost, sometimes after a time period you can get the copyrights reverted back to you. Do so by asking for them, and then sell the article to other markets and foreign publications.

If you cannot get your copyrights returned or if you don't want to hassle, return to your research, use the bubble method to brainstorm other angles, and come up with a retwisted slant and write a fresh query that will sell.

For more information on copyrights, review *Writer's Market* or other references for professional writers.

Fees and the Magazine Writer

We've talked about analyzing markets, sending one query a day, using the bubble method, formatting a manuscript and targeting your reader. The bottom line is that you need to make money in order to stay in business. Beginning writers know that, but experienced writers use various techniques to do it. Here are some proven methods:

• Negotiate: When you receive an assignment whether it's in a telephone call or in a letter, there's no rule that you must accept the amount offered or give up all your copyrights. You can get from ten to fifty percent more by asking; you can sell only the first serial rights; or ask for the copyright to be returned once the article has been published. You have to be bold, yet this approach does work.

Your professional approach increases your potential... see p.79

After you've established what the magazine is offering, write or call and ask, "Can your budget cover $50.00 (or some other amount) more?" What's the worst that can happen? Of course—the editor says, "No, that is our standard rate for first-time writers."

• The ball is in your court: You can look elsewhere and sell your article to another publication, or take the original amount. You can also ask: "Will the rate increase on future assignments? To how much?" Find out if the magazine pays for photos and/or illustrations separately.

Will the article you were assigned require many long distance calls for expert quotes or to verify facts? Will you be required to travel into the city to visit the Hall of Records, and so on? If that's the case, you may want to total your best estimate on the expenses and group them together when asking for reimbursement. You may want to ask for and negotiate travel and telephone expenses, and the cost of FAX or express mail service.

You Have
to Be a Business

W hen you forward an assigned article, make a habit of invoicing the magazine. They may or may not need the form you send. If they do and haven't told you, it's one less obstacle in the bookkeeping process. You'll get your check faster. If they don't use it, they'll merely credit you with efficiency.

You can buy fancy invoice forms at any office supply store, but this one works well. Be sure to keep a copy for your files, or keep it on computer disk. Enter the date you've invoiced the magazine in your records.

A sample invoice follows on the next page.

> *Invoice immediately, the sooner you send it, the sooner you get paid*

INVOICE

TO: The magazine's name/address

FROM: Your name/address/phone/social security number

DATE: Today's date

FOR: Be specific with article title, date assigned, editor's name and anything else that needs to be included for a speedy processing of your check

TOTAL $000.00

Always consult with an accountant for specifics on your business, what is deductible and what's not. But here are some practical recommendations:

You'll need a simple bookkeeping system, and you can use one of the computer software programs or do it the old-fashioned way. If you chose the traditional route, you'll need a journal in which to record the date, your income, magazine, the amount, the date the money was received, and the subject of the article. (A photocopy of the check you received for payment of your article, attached to your invoice and kept in that magazine's file is a handy reference for us, not-so-accurate bookkeepers.)

Stationery stores have bookkeeping journals for your receivables (money you've earned) and payables (expenses). Get them today. It's easier to keep the records up-to-date than to have to pull them all together at the end of the year.

Keep a daily calendar of where you go, the people you see, where you eat (if you're away on business), and the reason for the trip. This includes visits to the library, the university, the post office, copy store, and appointments with a magazine's editor or someone you're interviewing for an article or query. Check with your accountant, of course, as you may want to jot down the round trip mileage; some writers keep a travel journal in the glove compartment of their cars. If your records are ever audited by the IRS, your calendar will substantiate your activities and records for that year.

When talking to your tax preparer or accountant, find out if you need a separate checking account in order not to mingle your writing income from that of other sources. This is especially helpful come tax time as checks are often receipts. If you normally buy less expensive items using cash, consider a petty cash box, but do keep all your receipts.

The stationery store also sells telephone logs. If you're working with a number of magazines on a regular basis and your calls are reimbursed, or if you're using your home phone for business calls, a log in which you record all calls makes billing and record keeping much simpler. Or you can make your own log on a computer file or use a lined tablet.

So what's deductible? What's not?

Only business-related expenses are deductible. During an interview, if you meet an expert for a lunch meeting, that's a deduction. If you purchase a reference book (such as this one), turn a spare room into an office used exclusively for writing, that's a deduction. Buying equipment? A deduction. *Consumer Reports* magazine often has articles on what's deductible to use as a jumping off point, but always double check with your tax advisor.

The IRS has information on the requirements for deductions as well as quarterly self-employment filings. Review the information prior to April 15 and keep receipts on everything you purchase and life will be simpler and more organized. Public libraries also carry a wealth of tax information books and forms, but the librarians will not answer questions on deductions.

Writer's Little Helpers

What do you really need in order to be a writer? And in an office? Beginning writers usually function in the two extremes when it comes to a room of their own. Some rent a grand space in a high-rise building or totally renovate a room in their home and fill it with spiffy equipment. Some beginners slap a typewriter or computer on the kitchen counter and attempt to create salable work with the constant interruptions that situation provokes.

As an experienced writer, a space of your own will help your career. You needn't evict the kids from the TV room or pay a small fortune for space in a new office complex downtown. A corner of the bedroom or another quiet area can work just as well as long as you're comfortable leaving work in progress.

Most writers do have a room of their own. For some, it's a dream office with oak desk and filing cabinets. Others go the low-tech route and place a door, purchased from the home improvement warehouse, over two two-drawer filing cabinets and call it a desk. My office's decor is between the two: it's comfortable, attractive, and cozy, with a view of my roses, the palm trees swaying, and the animals from bunnies to birds who frequent my garden. Yes, and it has a door that shuts.

If you're beginning to set up or renovate your office, think bargains. Shop at garage sales for used furniture and scan the classified section of the paper for some great buys on desks, file cabinets, chairs, etc., even a fax, computer stuff, and accessories.

Here are the only prerequisites for a writer's office:

1. A place where you can concentrate, preferably with a door. While I know one writer who works in front of the television while the kids watch Barney and Sesame Street, there may be times when quiet is essential.

2. A surface for writing, one that will hold your computer

and printer, fax, modem, etc. and other high-tech necessities or a typewriter. Also adequate lighting for nights when you have to work after dark.

3. A shelf for books and reference materials.

4. Boxes, crates, filing cabinets. (I use all of these, and I make piles on the floor for whatever article, research or book I'm working on.)

5. A telephone.

6. A window, for ventilation and a view to look at while resting your eyes from the computer screen. Natural light is the best; good light is essential.

7. A large, office style wastepaper basket.

8. A chair that provides support for your back.

Budget permitting, extras to add:

1. FAX machine

2. Copy machine

3. Fan/air conditioner

4. Desk lamp

5. Answering machine

6. Visitor's chair or overstuffed chair in which to sit while editing articles.

7. Extra table.

8. "In" baskets. One that temporarily holds correspondence to be answered and another for filing.

Decorate your office so that it's comfortable and somewhat presentable. You'll be spending a good deal of time in there so make it a "feel good" place where you can create. Since I write books as well as magazine articles, I've framed the covers of my books. They decorate my office walls.

You may want to frame your favorite articles, hang posters of the Beatles, or Grandma's antique cross-stitch sampler.

Evaluating Software

What's the best software for a magazine writer? The one you'll use and be comfortable using. Talk to other writers in your network and at conferences. Barge in on writer friends, sit at their desk, and try out their software. Chat with people in your e-mail groups about the software they use for word processing. From accounting programs to file management programs, there's software for every need. If money is a concern, think small but buy what you need to succeed.

Learn to depend on your spelling program and the thesaurus that's part of the word processing program. The spelling one makes life easier, but remember that it only checks for incorrect words, see Chapter 9. The thesaurus can make your work dazzle—use it to avoid boring your reader.

Some writers love grammar programs; I don't. We have a mutual contempt for each other and when I use them, the articles I write turn out stiff and without that "Eva zing."

Unless it's built into your system, try out a grammar program before you install one. Granted, the programs do clean up grammar, but I think they draw the life out of creativity.

Purchase software (programs versus hardware, which is equipment) from a reputable store. Make sure the store gives you the toll-free phone number of the software manufacturer's "help line" or agrees to help you install it. If you're currently enrolled in college, check with the bookstore—you may find some excellent deals just for students.

Look for software reviews in computer and writing magazines, and as with all equipment, shop around. Programs do go on sale.

Organizing Your Home Office

There's no right way to organize your office, but experienced writers generally agree that keeping the books, paper, and equipment you use most often close at hand is sensible.

If you regularly use a library-sized dictionary, keep it close to your desk. If the view from your window is outstanding, move your desk so you can see it.

A note on telephones and answering machines. If you share your home and your telephone lines, consider a separate line for your office. When answering your "work" phone, duplicate how other professionals do it: "Good morning, this is Susan Smith." Or "Hello, George Wills speaking." It feels awkward at first, but announcing your name is a service. It lets the caller know who you are and gets you into a business frame of mind. You needn't tell the caller, an editor at a magazine you've been dying to write for, that you've just come in from dumping the trash. Pretend you're all business and use your best telephone manners when that phone rings. Answering your phone in a business manner also signals to well-meaning friends that you're working.

Ditto with the message you leave on the answering machine. Make it warm; make it business-like.

Keep it short, and always leave your phone number

A NOTE
OF THANKS

*T*hank you for spending this time with me and allowing me into your mind. If you were in my classroom or sitting here in my office, I'd finish with a few words of motivation so here they are:

You can do it. You *can* become a magazine writer who sells everything you write and writes everything you sell.

I hope you'll share some of the advice in these pages with others in your circle. I hope you'll stop and chat with me at the next writer's conference we both attend or you'll invite me to speak to the members of your writing group. I'll be looking forward to it.

Writing is a process. By writing every day, we become better writers. There's no quick and easy way to it. So keep sending out those queries; one a day will do. And if you'd like to share any of your success stories, write to me:

Eva Shaw, Ph.D. — Success Stories
Loveland Press
P. O. Box 7001
Loveland, CO 80537-0001

WRITER'S BOOKSHELF

T he following are some of the books I recommend to students, colleagues, and other writers. You can find lots of tips in writer's magazines, too. Browse at your bookstore, visit the library, talk with friends, find a local writing magazine or newsletter, or one geared for your specific interest area. In addition to a good (read that thick) dictionary and possibly a set of encyclopedias (or one on CD ROM), you'll probably want to own any of the writer's marketing guides, such as *Writer's Market* or *The Writer's Handbook*. Books are about $30.00, sometimes less at discount and membership stores.

The American Directory of Writer's Guidelines, John C. Mutchler. Quill Driver Books, Clovis, CA: 1998. A reference book that spells out for a writer exactly what magazine and book editors need—in the editors' own words.

The Complete Idiot's Guide to Creative Writing, Laurie E. Rozakis, Ph.D. New York: Alpha Books, 1997. A step-by-step guide to writing novels, plays and much more with down-to-earth advice on selling, too.

An Interactive Guide to the Internet, J. Michael Blocker, Vito Amato, and Jon Storslee. Indianapolis: Que E&T, 1996. A hands-on learning tool to help maneuver the information superhighway.

Internet Research Companion, Geoffrey W. McKim. Indianapolis: Que E&T, 1996. Offers skills to effectively use the Internet as a research tool.

The National Writers Union Guide to Freelance Rates & Standard Practice, Alexander Kopelman, Writer/Editor. Cincinnati, OH: National Writers Union, Writer's Digest Books, 1995.

The New Quotable Woman, compiled and edited by Elaine Partnow. New York: Meridian, 1993. The definitive treasury of notable words by women from Eve to the present.

The New Well-Tempered Sentence, Karen Elizabeth Gordon. Boston: Houghton Mifflin, 1993. A punctuation handbook for the innocent, the eager, and the doomed written in a "you can do it" tone that empowers even the grammatically challenged.

The Portable Writers Conference, Steven Mattee. Fresno, CA: Quill Driver Books, 1997. Great for information and even better for motivation. Everything in one source from writing to selling.

Protect Your Rights, Carole Williams. Sedalia, CO: Rainbow Creek Press. Discussion of rights for magazine writers. 14-page booklet.

The Quotable Quote Book, Merrit Malloy and Shauna Sorensen. New York: Citadel Press Book, 1990. A collection of funny, outrageous, and perfect quotes to add the right touch to words.

Romance Writers Phrase Book, Jean Kent and Candace Shelton. New York: Perigee, 1984. An essential source for any writer who wants to add romance to his/her work; contains over 3000 descriptive tags.

Sell More Books! Straight Talk on Marketing for Authors, Carole Williams. Sedalia, CO: Rainbow Creek Press. Booklet contains 26 pages packed with advice and examples from a professional publicist.

Simpson's Contemporary Quotations, James B. Simpson. Boston: Houghton Mifflin, 1988. A wealth of quotes and an excellent addition to any writer's library.

The Successful Writer's Guide to Writing the Non-Fiction Book, Including Tricks of the Trade, Eva Shaw. Loveland, CO: Loveland Press, 1999. A must-have collection of insider information and ways to make more money. It is essential if you want to prosper as a successful writer.

Time Management for the Creative Person, Lee Silber. New York: Random House, 1998. Tips and tricks to streamline any creative person's life and ways to make a living. Really life savers for those of us who use both sides of the brain.

Writer's Guide to Query Letters and Cover Letters, Gordon Burgett. Rocklin, CA: Prima, 1992. Sound advice, from an expert's perspective on how to get the most from query and cover letters.

Writer's Resource Guide to Workshops, Conferences, Artist's Colonies and Academic Programs, David Emblidge and Barbara Zheutlin. New York: Watson-Guptell, 1997. Check this book and inspire yourself with enrichment programs that will help hone the craft.

The Writer's Survival Guide, Rachel Simon. Cincinnati, OH: Story Press, 1997. An instructional, insightful guide to direct the new and seasoned writer on a variety of topics.

The Writers Sourcebook, Rachel Friedman Ballon. Los Angeles: Lowell House, 1996. A creativity sparker that helps to alleviate the frustration, chaos, and real and imagined suffering of writing.

Writing Your Life, Lou Willett Stanek, Ph.D. New York: Avon, 1996. A necessary book for anyone writing memoirs, essays, or feelingful material.

Motivational Books

The Artist's Way, Julia Cameron, 1992, New York: Jeremy P. Tarcher Publishers. This is *the* best book on sparking creative genius, risk taking, problem solving, and all around excellent creative advice.

Bird by Bird: Some Instructions on Writing and Life, Anne Lamott. New York: Pantheon, 1994. A classic writer's guide and a guidebook for what it means to be a writer.

The Courage to Write, Ralph Keyes, 1995, New York: Henry Holt. This must-have book ensures that writers of every level understand that writer's jitters are common; anxiety is an integral and even necessary part of the writing process.

Idea Catcher, editors of Story Press. Cincinnati, OH: Story Press, 1995. A journaling book for anyone who needs to take creative sparks and ignite their writing.

If You're Writing, Let's Talk, Joel Saltzman. Rocklin, CA: Prima, 1997. A slim and powerful book; it is a road map past writer's block.

poemcrazy (ed. the word is correct), Susan Goldsmith Woodridge. New York: Three River Press, 1996. An essential inspiration for anyone who has a poem lurking just beneath the surface.

Wild Mind: Living the Writer's Life, Natalie Goldberg. New York: Bantam, 1990. Exercises to spark creativity regardless of a writer's level of expertise.

Writing Down the Bones, Natalie Goldberg. Boston: Shambhala Publications, 1986. Thought-provoking and realistic, it's the right advice on the art and practice of writing.

Writing from Your Inner Self, Elaine Farris Hughes. New York: Harper Perennial, 1991. Sixty-three creative exercises written to stimulate artistic and original thought.

Writing in a Convertible with the Top Down, Kristi Killian and Sheila Bender. New York: Warner Books, 1992. Inspiration and information in a lively and informal form; gets a writer going even in the worst storms.

WRITER'S ORGANIZATIONS

*I*n addition to attending writing conferences and one-day workshops, every professional writer can benefit from being a member of one of the many writers' organizations. Write for information and select the one that's best for you. Do a search on-line; many of the writer's organizations are developing websites.

This list, keep in mind, is not complete because new organizations spring up all the time. For more writers' associations, check out the web (many have sites) or refer to the *Encyclopedia of Associations,* Gale Research Company, available at most libraries.

AMERICAN MEDICAL WRITERS ASSOCIATION
9650 Rockville Pike
Bethesda, MD 20814

AMERICAN SOCIETY OF JOURNALISTS AND AUTHORS,
INC.
1501 Broadway, Suite 302,
New York, NY 10036

ASSOCIATED WRITING PROGRAMS
Tallwood House, Mail Stop 1E3
Fairfax, VA 22030

AUTHORS GUILD (and AUTHORS LEAGUE OF AMERICA)
330 W. 42nd Street
New York, NY 10036

DOG WRITERS OF AMERICA, INC.
173 Union Road
Coatesville, PA 19320

HORROR WRITERS ASSOCIATION
P. O. Box 423
Oak Forest, IL 60452

INTERNATIONAL BLACK WRITERS
P. O. Box 1030
Chicago, IL 60690

INTERNATIONAL P.E.N. WOMEN WRITERS' COMMITTEE
523 W. 11th St. No. 75
New York, NY 10024

INTERNATIONAL WOMEN'S WRITING GUILD
Box 810, Gracie Station
New York, NY 10028-0082

NATIONAL WRITERS ASSOCIATION
1450 S. Havana, Suite 424
Aurora, CO 80012

NATIONAL WRITERS UNION
13 Astor Place, 7th Floor
New York, NY 10003

PEN AMERICAN CENTER
568 Broadway
New York, NY 10012

PEN CENTER U.S.A. WEST
672 Lafayette Park Pl., No. 41
Los Angeles, CA 90057

SOCIETY OF CHILDREN'S BOOK WRITERS
AND ILLUSTRATORS
22736 Vanowen St., Suite 106
West Hills, CA 93107

TEXT AND ACADEMIC AUTHORS ASSOCIATION
Box 535
Orange Springs, FL 32182-0535

WESTERN WRITERS OF AMERICA
6309 Caminito del Pastel
San Diego, CA 92111-6825

WRITING ACADEMY
267 Maple St.
New Wilmington, PA 16142

Index

*Page numbers in bold type
indicate where definitions occur.*

$\mathscr{I}$

$\mathscr{K}$

$\mathscr{L}$

$\mathscr{M}$

$\mathscr{N}$

$\mathscr{O}$

Notes

Notes

Notes

Fill these
Pages Up!

Notes

Notes

Fill these Pages Up!